HINDUISM

A complete introduction to this ancient religious tradition.

HINDUISM

The Eternal Law
An Introduction to the Literature, Cosmology and Cults of the Hindu Religion

by

MARGARET STUTLEY

AQUARIAN

THE AQUARIAN PRESS
Wellingborough, Northamptonshire

First published 1985

For Beryl

British Library Cataloguing in Publication Data

Stutley, Margaret
Hinduism: the eternal law: an introduction to the literature, cosmology and cults of the Hindu religion.
1. Hinduism
I. Title
294.5 BL1202

ISBN 0-85030-348-6

The Aquarian Press is part of the Thorsons Publishing Group

Printed and bound in Great Britain

Contents

Introduction

Hinduism is the name given by Europeans to the religious, cultural, social, political and philosophical beliefs which make up the totality of the Hindu way of life. Hindus themselves call their religious tradition 'the eternal law' (*sanatana dharma*) which has existed for over five thousand years, a period matched only by the unbroken cultural development of China.

Hinduism spread far outside India to become, until the thirteenth century AD, the main religious force in south-east Asia. Some of its tenets may still be traced in the Mahayana Buddhism of those countries. Later it spread westwards to East Africa, the West Indies, Europe and the United States of America.

Classical (or modern) Hinduism acquired its characteristic form soon after the period of the *Upanisads* (about 800 to 400 BC). Theoretically the Vedic religion (an ancient sacrificial cult based on the Vedas) forms its basis, but in fact it is only one of the main factors in a long and ever-evolving cultural synthesis. In common with all other religions, Hinduism is a syncretistic product — the notion of a pure religion exists only in the imagination of its adherents. The Vedic religion was brought to India by the Aryan-speaking peoples who, in the second millennium BC, migrated from the Caucasian steppes. Some groups settled in Anatolia, others in Iran, north-west India, Greece, Italy and Western Europe. The first wave of Aryans reached India about 1700 BC, and later were followed by a number of other groups until about 800 BC.

Although the fair-skinned Aryans considered themselves much superior to the dark-skinned natives, the Dravidian and Indus Valley civilizations were culturally far in advance of the incomers. But the Aryans had the advantage when it came to warfare and weapons.

A number of Vedic beliefs still remain in modern Hinduism, but there are also differences. In Vedism the priests were the dominant class, but there were no temples or images and little, if any, devotional type of religion. The priests strongly opposed the phallic worship which was then prevalent in some of the indigenous cults and which later came to the fore in the Hindu cult of Siva. But many Vedic elements still remain in the domestic and initiatory rites of the upper classes.

Hinduism, or more properly the Hindu Tradition, is an aggregation of innumerable religious beliefs, of cults, of customs and of rituals. It cannot be treated as a single religion since it has no founder, no one sacerdotal order to institute set dogmas, and no central organization. Today, Hindu priests function mainly in a private and domestic capacity.

The vast range and complexity of cultic practices cannot be described in one, or for that matter, many volumes. But it is hoped that this very brief and much simplified outline will encourage those interested in the religious thought of the world to study this ancient tradition more deeply — a tradition that encompasses the thoughts and spiritual strivings of countless mystics and original thinkers over thousands of years, and which is one of the highest spiritual achievements of mankind.

The innumerable deities, myths, rituals and symbols may be interpreted in various ways, according to the individual worshipper's level of understanding, and hence Hinduism may be said to be 'all things to all men'. So diverse are these cults that outside India they would be regarded as separate religions. In fact, the Hindu Tradition includes all types of religious belief known to man, which accounts for its dynamism, resilience, tolerance, and ability to amalgamate the most disparate beliefs. In it may be found the worship of ancestors; of cosmic elements; of Mother goddesses; of deified culture heroes; of animals, birds and snakes; of trees and plants; of sacred stones; of countless godlings, spirits, ghosts and celestial beings; of high gods such as Varuna, Visnu and Siva; and the worship of God in feminine form. Apart from polytheism, Hinduism also includes monotheistic, monist, and even atheistic views. These varied approaches are possible because Divine Reality is the transcendent-immanent ground of everything and therefore may be contacted at all levels, in all places, and in all things.

The diverse (and sometimes contradictory) beliefs and views stem from the meeting of different races and cultures: these include the Deccan Neolithic (dating from about 2000 to 750 BC); the Dravidian, which contributed so greatly to the development of Hinduism, especially in relation to the later devotional cults; the tribal and aboriginal groups (only partly assimilated to Hinduism) which constitute the lowest stratum of society; and the Aryan culture. From the interaction of these groups arose a vast, uncoordinated mass of new and continually changing religious beliefs and practices, some being developed, others modified, and others almost, but not quite, disappearing. Anything that has even a vestige of religious significance is never discarded and may come again to the fore centuries later. Thus no single religious system can be said to represent Hinduism in its entirety.

Such a variety of religious views accounts for the tolerant attitude of the majority of Hindus to the beliefs of others. To the Indian mind every single thing possesses some divine potentiality and Ultimate Reality lies beyond the limitations, artificial divisions and differences of individual cults whose followers all strive for liberation in different ways.

The main belief deriving from the Veda, and which is common to most Hindu cults, is that one immanent-transcendent Unity exists behind and beyond the apparent multiplicity of the universe. This view parallels that of modern atomic scientists who calculate that everything in the universe evolved from a region billions of times smaller than a single proton, one of the atom's basic particles. Similarly, molecular biologists have revealed the underlying unity of all forms and have pointed out that the fundamental molecules of a cabbage, fly or bacterium, are the same as those of man. The Indian Nobel Prize winner, Sir Jayadish Chandra Bose, based his scientific investigations on the ancient Indian teaching that whatever can be found in man and animal must also be traceable in vegetal life. Another Indian Nobel Prize winner, the crystallographer C. V. Raman, based his work on the tenet that so-called animate and inanimate stones are imbued with the mysterious force (*brahman*) that gives life, and he demonstrated that crystals, having assumed a certain shape, undergo continuous change from growth to decay.

Over the centuries Hinduism has sometimes flourished, at other times declined only to recover again, but with the intrusions of the Moslems the high Hindu culture began a long downward trend allowing many negative and pessimistic elements to enter it which were not apparent during the earlier Vedic times. The Moslems met little opposition from the armies of the Hindu kingdoms, who failed to unite in the face of the common enemy. The intruders destroyed the magnificent temples of North India, images, and everything of a religious nature that they could lay their hands on. Buddhism also disappeared from India at this time, the huge Buddhist monasteries with their thousands of monks being easy prey for the iconoclasts who quickly and mercilessly massacred the unarmed inhabitants and razed the buildings: yet Hinduism survived.

By the time of the British occupation Hinduism was at a very low ebb, but later was stimulated by the work of a number of British orientalists. These included: Charles Wilkins (1749-94), a brilliant linguist, who recognized the relationship of European languages to Persian and totally rejected the current view, based on the Bible, that all languages derived from Hebrew and became garbled at the Tower of Babel; Henry Colebrooke (1765-1837); H. H. Wilson (1789-1860); and a number of others, including French and German Indologists. Many Hindu Sanskrit texts were translated into European languages, and the study of Sanskrit was encouraged. It is an Indo-European language closely related to Hittite, Old (Avestan) Persian, Greek, Latin, ancient Slav, Armenian, and to the Germanic and Celtic tongues.

Today, enormous problems confront Indian civilization. In addition to centuries of alien rule (for the Moslems were as much intruders as the British), there are the immense problems of over-population, soil infertility, poverty and mass illiteracy. Fortunately Hinduism possesses the necessary dynamism to expand, modify and adapt to the ever-changing socio-religious conditions and needs, today and in the future, as it has during the past five thousand years.

1. The Veda

The term *Veda* (literally, 'knowledge') refers to divine, as distinct from mundane, knowledge 'seen' by the ancient inspired seers (*rsis*), and hence these collections of texts are termed *sruti* 'revealed'. The Veda comprises a vast body of sacred literature which developed over many centuries and originally was transmitted orally in an extraordinarily efficient manner.

Originally there were three Vedas: the *Rgveda, Samaveda* and *Yajurveda* known collectively as the 'threefold knowledge'. Later the more magically orientated *Atharvaveda* was added as well as the Brahmanas, Aranyakas and *Upanisads.* For over three thousand years the Veda has been the fount of much of the spiritual, social and cultural life of India and it enables us to understand more of the later teachings contained in the Hindu Tradition. Vedic mythology is especially interesting as it 'forms a connecting link between the later Indian phase of religious beliefs and the Indo-Iranian as well as the earliest Indo-European phase'.[1]

The Vedas contain many disparate and imperfectly synthesized tribal beliefs and cults as well as advanced spiritual teachings. The oldest, the *Rgveda* (Veda of praise), is by far the most interesting, although it is impossible to date exactly the beginning of its compilation since Hindus regard their religion as eternal. It appears to have been composed over a long period up to about 900 BC. Some Indologists consider that it belongs to a period prior to the Aryan intrusion into India; others, to a period between 1400 and 1000 BC when the incomers had settled in the Punjab. The oldest hymns are contained in Books II to VII, the latest in Books I and X.

A number of diverse creation myths and types of religious belief are contained in the Vedas, including polytheism, dualism, monotheism and monism. One hymn in the *Rgveda* (1.64) is monist and states that there is only One Principle or Absolute, the sexless, attributeless Real (*sat*), the Unity containing the world and all its myriads of creatures, which is called by many different names: Indra, Mitra, Varuna, etc. Another monistic hymn states that in the beginning there was neither existence nor non-existence, neither mortals nor immortals, neither life nor death, only a formless void of non-manifestation over which the One primordial entity 'breathed by its own nature'. One hymn (10,129) states that the gods are later than the world's creation although no one knows its inception. Dualistic metaphysics appear in 10.82, which states that the Waters contained the primeval germ from which rose Visvakarman, the first-born of the universe and fashioner of the world from existing eternal matter. Elsewhere it is said that Brahmanaspati (the special intermediary of the gods and priests), produced the world by blast and smelting like a smith (10.72,2), but in verse six the gods are said to have kicked up a thickening cloud of dust as if dancing and then caused all things to grow. In 10.90 the First Principle is the Cosmic Man (*purusa*), a kind of giant in whose vast body the world and heaven are contained. When he was sacrificed the universe and its inhabitants came into being and hence he is both the material source and the creator and transcender of the world process. Another hymn relates that creation arose from heat (*tapas*) giving rise successively to Eternal Law and Truth, night, sea and the Year (which signifies Totality), after which the 'secondary' creator Dhatar formed sun and moon, heaven and earth, and so on. A fragment of an ancient myth contained in 10.10 relates that the origin of human beings was from the first pair of twins Yama and Yami; whereas the later *Atharvaveda* (19.53,5f) contains the philosophical notion that Time (*kala*) is the first cause of all existence: 'Time begot yonder heaven . . . also these earths. That which was, and that which shall be, urged forth by Time, spreads out. Time created the earth, in Time the sun burns. In Time are all beings . . .' The same Veda refers to periodic creations, implying that creation is not produced out of nothing, as in the Semitic religions, but from already existing matter. Other hymns attribute creation to various deities, and in *Rgveda* 10.41,7 the universe is said to be the finished product of a skilled carpenter: 'What was the wood, which the tree, out of which they fashioned heaven and earth?'

Although the Aryans practised some agriculture their economy was mainly based on cattle as the chief source of food and of by-products useful to man. Cattle were also the principal form of currency. So important were cattle that the cow was eulogized and a heavenly origin attributed to it; none the less cows were sometimes sacrificed, and thus the *Aitareya Brahmana* (1.15) states that a cow that miscarries may be slaughtered for a king or other important person. The Vedic Aryans also ate beef but milch cows were never slaughtered, only barren cows and calves. It was customary also to slaughter a cow in funeral rites: a male corpse was covered with a cow hide as this was believed to possess inherent protective and revivifying powers. A live cow was presented also to the officiating priest, and the same animal was supposed to carry the deceased over the dread river Vaitarani which forms the boundary between this world and the next. A variant of this belief spread to northern Europe where formerly it was thought that one who gave a cow to the poor would be guided to heaven by the same animal. In Lancashire the Milky Way was called the 'cow's lane' — the way the dead entered heaven.[2] The deep veneration accorded this animal further increased when it became identified with Aditi, the goddess of the abundance of nature and infinite expansion. In Hinduism cow slaughter is strictly prohibited.

The Aryans spoke disparagingly of the natives and described them as black-skinned, noseless and as phallic worshippers. They endeavoured to keep themselves apart but over the years inter-marriage and cultural exchanges inevitably took place, a fact borne out by the large number of non-Aryan words in the Vedic Sanskrit vocabulary.

A wholesome joy of life shines through the *Rgveda*; it is without any of the extreme world-weariness so prevalent later among some intellectuals, and which culminated in the ideal of the homeless mendicant devoid of possessions and mundane attachments. Some hymns show a love of music, dancing, drinking and gambling, although the last is disapproved of by the priests. Desire for immortality is not stressed as being attained through one's descendants, but rather longevity in this world is desired — the God-ordained lifetime being 'one hundred autumns'. People are encouraged to live 'full lives' and to 'find old age delightful'. Death does not seem to have been feared, for the dead follow the path trodden by Yama — the first man to die. Yama, as a deity, belongs 'to the Indo-Iranian prehistoric period. He is identical with Yima who, in the *Avesta*, is the first human being, the primeval ancestor of the human race'.[3] Yama provides a comfortable and pleasant abode where there will be happy reunions with loved ones and friends and all evil, disease and misery left behind. In this realm the deceased will be endowed with a new and glorious body. It appears that corpses were usually burnt, but during the earliest times burial was customary among Indo-Europeans.

Among the older gods of the *Rgveda* is Varuna, the embodiment of kingship and the supreme moral ruler who, by the time of the compilation of the *Rgveda* had superseded Dyaus, the ancient Indo-European sky god. Varuna is implored to forgive sins: 'If we have sinned against the man who loves us, have ever wronged a brother, friend, comrade/ The neighbour ever with us, or a stranger, O Varuna, remove from us the trespass/ If we, as gamesters cheat at play, [have] done wrong unwittingly or sinned of purpose/ Cast all these sins away like loosened fetters, and, Varuna, let us be thine own beloved'. Varuna also establishes and fixes the paths of sun and moon, the cycle of the seasons, and prevents the ocean overflowing. With his noose (*pasa*) he binds wrongdoers or afflicts them with paralysis or dropsy. His followers live in awe of him for, though predominantly just, his ways are inscrutable. He is closely associated with the cosmic waters which alone existed in the beginning. All creatures who drown go to his realm. But despite his high standing he too was in decline towards the end of the Vedic period, although still closely connected with two highly important religious concepts, namely *rta* (cosmic and moral order) and *maya* (the creative and transforming power of a deity).

Rta refers to 'the immanent dynamic order or inner balance of the cosmic manifestations themselves',[4] as well as to divine law, truth, morality and virtuous conduct. Sin results from the violation of *rta* in the moral, ritual and sacrificial sphere. *Rta* is regarded as a concrete material entity which subsequently was replaced by the related principle of *dharma*. The ideal virtuous life is one lived in accordance with Varuna's ordinances, in harmony with friends, neighbours and strangers.

The other term *maya* means 'to measure' out all visible forms which, being relative, are necessarily transitory. *Maya* is a mighty power, for by it Varuna 'measured out', that is created, the firmament; by *maya* Indra overcame Vrtra; and other high gods also 'measured out' forms and beings. Basically *maya* is a neutral force and therefore can be directed to good or bad ends. In the *Rgveda*, *maya* appears as a kind of 'occult power', and in the same work is used in the sense of a magic 'show' or 'illusion'. Some 1500 years later this notion developed into the Vedantic concept of the illusory nature of the cosmos, regarded as an ephemeral series of changes devoid of ultimate reality, since only the Ultimate Real is permanent. This concept is also common to some Mahayana Buddhist schools.

Varuna is closely associated with the benevolent solar deity Mitra (identical with the ancient Iranian god Mithra) whose origin can be traced back to the second millennium BC. The original meaning of the name was 'contract' and later 'friend'. Mitra oversees and guards men's contracts and, when associated with the god Aryaman, functions as the protector of Aryan society. He is also associated with Bhaga who gives human beings their share of happiness. The name Bhaga means 'sharer or dispenser' and was also an epithet applied to a tribal chieftain who, according to ancient Aryan custom, annually distributed the communal produce of the tribe to its adult members. The gods mentioned above, and some others, are called Adityas, sons of the goddess Aditi, 'unbounded' whose nature is manifested 'in any expansion of phenomenal life'.[5]

Another important Vedic deity was Indra, to whom over 250 hymns are addressed. Initially Indra was a weather and storm god, the archetype of the world's generative forces, and hence he was said to have a 'thousand testicles'. Later he became the mighty war god of the Aryans and the heroic ideal of warriors, the protector of the 'Aryan colour', the subjugator of enemies. However, Agni, — the deification of fire — is ritually far more important than Indra, fire being an essential factor in the Vedic sacrificial system.

Indra's close companions are the Maruts (storm spirits) who, on the mythological plane, reflect 'the Indo-Iranian societies of young warriors' (*marya*).[6] Urged on by the exhilarating effects of the sacred *soma* juice Indra overcame the enemies of the Aryans, including the dragon Vrtra who held back the waters (a common mythological theme occurring in many cultures). The dragon represents the forces of chaos or non-manifestation which must be mastered before the world can be established and thus Indra, after his victory, is said to have created the earth and sky and then separated them. Despite Indra's importance in Vedic times his worship declined considerably in classical Hinduism.

According to some of the hymns it appears that even at that early date sceptics existed among the Aryan peoples. Some doubted that the gods had bodies; others doubted the very existence of the gods. Thus the creation hymn (*Rgveda* 5.129) ends with the following words:

> Who knoweth it forsooth, who can declare it here/ Whence this creation has arisen, whence it came?/ The gods came hither by this world's creation only;/ Who knoweth then, whence this creation has arisen?/ . . . whether it has been made or not: He who surveys/ This world in highest heaven, he may be knoweth,/ Or it may be, knoweth not.

In the same hymn the creative principle is unnamed and called 'the One', so 'already . . . the great idea of Universal Unity is foreshadowed, the idea that everything we see in Nature and which popular belief designates as 'gods', in reality is only the emanation of the One and Only One, that all plurality is only imaginary'.[7]

The prominent Vedic cult of fire is an Indo-Iranian institution stemming from prehistoric times. The sacrificial fire, the sun and lightning are deified and called Agni (fire). Agni is the mediator between gods and men, as well as the conveyor of the sacrificial offerings to the deities and burner of the impenetrable forests to provide space for his worshippers to settle. In his flesh-devouring form (*kravyad*) Agni burns corpses on the funeral pyres; by the head of asceticism (*tapas*) he blasts those who use ritual for evil ends. He is the priest of the gods and god of the priests; he joins heaven, earth and sky; he is the honoured guest in every home and demon-expeller *par excellence*, probably because demons were supposed to be especially active in darkness. Of all the gods only Agni is immortal and ever-young, being born anew from the fire sticks (*aranis*) with every kindling. Being immortal himself he possesses the capacity to confer immortality on his worshippers. He is simultaneously one, as deity, and many, as all individual fires.

Another ritually important deity was Soma (the Iranian *haoma*), the deification of the plant of the same name. Its juice was the essential libation at all Vedic sacrifices as well as a hallucinogenic drink for the worshippers. Thus both Agni and Soma had their basis in the divinized cult objects associated with the sacrificial system. The priests erected a mass of imagery round the simple process of pressing and straining the juice of the *soma* plant through a woollen filter. It is called the 'drink of immortality' and its exhilarating effects were stressed. Ecstatic visions were experienced and also feelings of superhuman strength and communion with the gods. *Soma* was Indra's favourite drink that enabled him to overcome enemies. In later Hinduism the *soma* ritual declined in importance largely because the technique of producing the liquor was lost and the actual plant forgotten.

Although the original plant is unknown, a number of suggestions have been put forward by Indologists and others. The independent researches of J. M. Allegro (*The Sacred Mushroom and the Cross*), and R. G. Wasson (*Soma, Divine Mushroom of Immortality*) into the fly agaric mushroom (*Amanita muscaria*) show that its hallucinogenic effects closely resemble the descriptions of the effects produced by drinking the *soma* juice. The mushroom grows in Europe and Afghanistan, but not on the plains of India. If the mushroom is really the *soma* plant, then when the Aryans settled in India, it would have been difficult to obtain and so various substitutes would have been used. Attempts were also made to attain the same ecstatic uplift by other methods, including extreme ascetic, orgiastic, mystical and yogic practices.

Among the many deities mentioned in the *Rgveda* some were already in decline when the work was compiled. Others later lost their high status, including Usas, the rosy goddess of the Dawn; the wind god, Vayu; the rain god, Parjanya; the sun gods, Surya and Savitr; Pusan, the ancient pastoral god of the ways, and guide of the dead; and the twin Asvins, the divine physicians. On the other hand, minor Vedic gods such as Visnu and Rudra/Siva became the high gods of classical Hinduism.

Rudra was a mysterious and much-feared deity who, despite being the tutelary deity of healing herbs, could send arrows that brought disease and death to man and animal; hence the propitiatory euphemism *siva*, auspicious, was applied to him. Later it became the proper name of the great god Siva who retains many of the ambivalent characteristics associated with Rudra.

Some Vedic gods are deifications of natural phenomena, others are abstractions personified, such as Sraddha (Faith) and Manyu (Anger). Many minor beings are mentioned, including the elf-like Rbhus, the nymph-like Apsarases, and hosts of sylvan and field spirits. Countless demons and other uncanny spirits are referred to as the enemies of the gods; sometimes the Aryans regarded the indigenes as demonic, probably because of their magical practices and knowledge of curative and poisonous herbs.

Among all the *Rgvedic* verses the most sacred is the *gayatri* addressed to the sun god: 'Let us think on the lovely splendour of the god Savitr that he may inspire our minds,' a passage repeated daily by most Hindus and at all rites and religious ceremonies.

The *Samaveda* (the name is derived from *saman*, a 'song' or 'melody') is the second of the four collections of Vedic hymns. The songs are mostly taken from the eighth and ninth books of the *Rgveda* and arranged according to the order in which they were chanted by a specific group of priests at the *soma* sacrifice. There are four collections of chants that resemble Western medieval plainsong in style and which are similarly based on a heptatonic scale.[8] One of the *Brahmanas* appended to the *Samaveda*, the *Samavidhana*, includes a manual of magic prescribing spells to be sung for specific purposes.

The third collection, the *Yajurveda*, consists mostly of prayers and sacrificial formulas addressed to various 'divinized' instruments used in the Vedic sacrifices. It is primarily a guide for the use of the Adhvaryu priest who performed the manual part of the ritual. The *Yajurveda* also contains ritual elements borrowed from the *Rgveda* supplemented by material associated with the many new ceremonies and complex rites that were being devised. The *Yajurveda* has two forms: the *Black* and the *White Yajurveda*. Included in the *Yajurveda* is the ceremony of the *Vajapeya* (Drink of Strength), a sacrifice offered by the nobility and connected with a chariot race. Another important ceremony was the *Rajasuya*, originally the inauguration of a king, but later performed annually to renew and quicken the royal energy on which the prosperity of the country depended. This ancient belief, common to many cultures, derives from the notion that by means of sacrifice the sacrificer himself is ritually 'reborn'. During the *Rajasuya* the king took part in a ritual dice game played with five dice representing the five seasons, and this the king always won, thereby symbolically bringing prosperity to the five regions. In another part of the ceremony he drove a quadriga into the middle of a herd of cows, and, touching one with his bow, took to himself the vigour of the herd (*Satapatha Brahmana* 5.4.3,1ff).

The *Yajurveda* also contains prayers and formulas for the building of the fire altar, a complex esoteric rite lasting for a year. The altar itself is equated with the fire god Agni, and consisted of 10,800 bricks in the form of a huge bird with outstretched wings. Much symbolism was associated with the bricks, the sacrificial implements and with everything connected with the altar.

The many names and laudatory epithets applied to each deity in the *Yajurveda* were thought to influence the gods favourably towards man and culminated in the thousand or more names of Siva and Visnu. The single sacred syllables (*bijas*) are also included; these were uttered at specific parts of the sacrifice. Many *bijas* were taken over by later Indian cults and are also known as mantras (magic formulas) whereas the original meaning referred to the sacred verses and sacrificial formulas of the four Vedas. One of the earliest *bijas* was *svaha*, usually translated into English as 'hail!' and uttered when gifts were offered to ancestors. The most sacred of all *bijas* is *OM.* It possesses enormous mystical significance, so much so that the *Upanisads* identify it with the impersonal *brahman* (*Katha Upanisad*, 2.16). *OM* is never used in ordinary conversation and has no profane meaning, but symbolizes the whole body of Hindu ideology in condensed form.

The *Atharvaveda* (of which there are two widely differing recensions) is the last of the four collections of the Vedic hymns. It is quite different from the other three Vedas and for a long time was not included in the Veda because it has little connection with sacrificial ritual. It also contained, among other things, many popular folk beliefs as well as spells to destroy enemies, to protect cattle and crops, to attract women, and to protect the belongings of priests. Other spells are used, in connection with curative herbs, which provide an insight into early Indian medicinal practices (*ayurveda*), later to be developed by Caraka (first century AD). Apart from the above it also possesses some hymns of great poetic beauty. Some of its contents appear to be older than the *Rgveda* and so provide an insight into the continuity, modifications and elaborations of Indian speculative views. There is also evidence that non-Aryan elements were already being absorbed during the Vedic period.

The name *Atharvaveda* means the 'Veda of the Atharvans' or the 'knowledge of magic formulas'. The Atharvans were a class of priestly magicians corresponding to the people of the Iranian *Avesta.* The Atharvans 'were still like the Shamans of Northern Asia and . . . the American Indians, "priests of magic", that is, priest and wizard combined in one person, as in the word "Magi" — as the Atharvans in Medea were called — the ideas of wizard and priest are merged together'.[9]

The *Atharvaveda* was closely connected with the warrior caste and therefore contains mantras relating to the protection and consecration of kings, for victory over enemies and battle charms. Two hymns are dedicated to the War Drum, the sound of which rallies the warriors, ensures victory and terrifies enemies. In much later times the War Drum became a divinized cult object in southern India.

The *Atharvaveda* is specially valuable in that it preserves a number of religious ideas not found in other Vedic texts, and represents the secular and intellectual aspects of ancient Indian civilization when still only slightly 'brahmanized'. Many of the spells, songs and formulas 'may be traced back to the Indo-European period . . . German and Indian magic songs thus give us a clue to a kind of prehistoric poetry of the Indo-Europeans'.[10] A number of exorcist and black magic formulas also are included in the *Atharvaveda* and the *Yajurveda*, and were used, as were some of the Christian Psalms, to curse enemies.

The Atharvanic folklore includes the widespread belief that diseases are caused by worms, a view also held by the ancient Sumerians, Babylonians, Egyptians, by the present-day Marsh Arabs of Iraq, and others. 'The worm which is in the entrails, that which is in the head, and that which is in the ribs . . . these worms we crush with this spell. The worms that have settled down in the hills, in the woods, in the plants, in the cattle, in the waters, and those which have settled down in our bodies, this whole breed of worms I crush' (*Atharvaveda* 2,31).

The *Brahmanas* dating from about 1000 BC onwards are ritual texts appended to the Vedas. They deal primarily with minute details of the sacrificial system and hence are concerned more with the externals of religion than with its spirit.

With the elaboration of the sacrificial cultus the priests' power increased and they arrogated to themselves more and more privileges. Such rights included the taking of other men's wives, and the right to have every barren cow presented to them; and in disputes between a brahmin and a non-brahmin the judgement was always to be given in favour of the brahmin, irrespective of the evidence. At the same time the status of women sank much lower than during Rgvedic and Upanisadic times. As with the early Christian Fathers and in Buddhist monasticism, women were greatly feared and regarded as evil and dangerous. Similarly the authors of the *Brahmanas* equated women with Nirrti — the goddess personifying evil and destruction — and stated that 'the woman, the Sudra, the dog and the crow are falsehood' (*Satapatha Brahmana* 14.1.1,31).

The most interesting of the *Brahmanas* is the *Satapatha* (attached to the *White Yajurveda*). It contains much sacrificial ritual and also numerous customs, practices and folklore. The compilers of the *Brahmanas* made sacrifice into an end in itself and personified and identified it with the creator Prajapati. Everything connected with sacrifice was imbued with immense magical potency. Sacrifice can be performed for good or bad ends according to the intention of the officiants. Thus evil effects can be directed against enemies, or priests may injure an ungenerous sacrificer by performing the rites in reverse order (as in the so-called Black Mass of European witchcraft). Later the performance of the huge, expensive and wasteful sacrifices declined and the idea was promulgated that the powers to be gained from successful sacrificing could also be attained by other means, such as extreme asceticism (*tapas*), which gave powers so great that even the gods feared great ascetics.

A number of disparate creation legends are included in both the *Brahmanas* and the *Rgveda.* Sometimes Prajapati is the only creator, elsewhere he himself is said to have been created. According to the *Satapatha Brahmana* (11.1.6,1ff), creation occurred when the primeval waters desired to propagate themselves. By extreme asceticism they heated themselves, whereupon a golden egg formed in the Waters which drifted about for a year. Then the 'secondary' creator Prajapati (whose lifetime was limited to 1,000 years) appeared. He broke open the golden egg and produced from it worlds, seasons, atmosphere, sky, and everything else. Then, knowing that his lifetime was limited, he desired to have progeny and placed reproductive energy in himself. From his mouth the gods emerged in light: with the 'breath of life which is below' he created demons and immediately knew, by the darkness that descended, that he had created evil for himself. Then he caused evil to overtake the demons. Another myth relates that creation arose from the non-existent (*a-sat*); yet another related that it sprang from the impersonal *brahman.*

The complex ritualism prescribed in the *Brahmanas* and the overwhelming arrogance of the priests, as well as the rise of the heterodox religions of Jainism and Buddhism, both of which rejected the Veda and the authority of the priesthood, finally brought a reaction. Jainism greatly intensified ascetic disciplines and taught that all things should be reverenced, including human and animal life, the immanent life of plants, fire, earth, water and wind. Buddhism advocated a less onerous discipline, but stressed the need for compassion for all creatures as well as pointing out the utter futility and cruelty of the sacrificial system. The *Aranyakas* (Forest Texts), appendices of the *Brahmanas,* also rejected the physical performance of sacrifice and instead interpreted it symbolically. These texts also include esoteric and mystical matters forbidden to the uninitiated which were transmitted secretly in forests and other secluded places.

Although the thirteen principal *Upanisads* (probably composed about 800 to 400 BC) are connected nominally with the *Brahmanas,* they did not originate from the priestly class but were composed by members of the warrior caste who, in times of peace, devoted themselves to religio-philosophical studies and discussions. Brahmins also engaged in a certain amount of philosophical speculation, but the *Aranyakas* and *Upanisads* (which constitute the end of Vedic literature), mark the real starting point of purely speculative thinking in India. A number of later works are also called *Upanisads* but they lack 'canonical' status.

Six *Upanisads* contain the original form of the Vedanta doctrine and are: the *Aitareya, Brhadaranyaka, Chandogya, Taittiriya, Kausitaki* and *Kena.* A further six, the *Katha, Svetasvatara, Maha Narayana, Isa, Mundaka* and *Prasna,* also contain Vedantic doctrines in addition to Samkhya and Yogic teachings and monotheistic views; but all the texts show signs of modifications and interpolations. None the less the *Upanisads* form the basis of all the Hindu philosophical systems and most of the religious traditions. A number of Upanisadic concepts gradually filtered down to some of the lower strata of Indian society and moderated many savage tribal practices.

As stated above, the philosophical views expressed in the *Upanisads* are not of one school and consequently are not consistent since they represent the thoughts and speculations of many men of diverse backgrounds and living in various periods. But the *Upanisads* provide a marvellous insight into the life and culture of the ancient Indian kingdoms, where priests, wandering teachers, learned women and others took part in public debates before the king, who was often a man of great learning.

The main teaching of the genuine *Upanisads* may be summed up in the sentence: 'The universe is the Brahman but the Brahman is the Atman,' which in modern words is equal to: 'The world is God, and God is my soul.'[11] Therefore the *atman* concept cannot be separated from the *brahman* principle. The identification of *brahman/atman* is a synthesis between *brahman* as the pervading and sustaining power of the world, and the teaching of yoga and inner meditation which attempts to induce the experience of ultimate reality within the individual. But *brahman/atman* is not exclusive to man for it is present in all living creatures and things.

The exact etymology of the term *brahman* is unknown. In the Veda it occurs many times in the sense of 'prayer', 'holy knowledge', or 'magic formula', by which man attempts to influence divine beings for his own ends. When these formulas were gathered together in the three Vedas it was known as the 'three-fold knowledge' and for a brief period was also called *brahman*, thereby equating it with sacred knowledge. In Upanisadic speculation it came to mean the holy power pervading the whole universe, and finally the creative principle itself, the one source of all existence. Thus it is equivalent to the Absolute or God. In some *Upanisads brahman* is regarded as a personal God or Isvara, a notion adopted by theists such as Ramanuja, Madhva and others who propounded a devotional type of religion. The etymology of *atman* is also uncertain but its meaning in the texts is clear. It refers to the inner eternal 'Self' or soul underlying the psycho-physical processes. It is different from an individual's mentality since in Indian thought the mind is regarded as a subtle form of matter illuminated by the self which is pure consciousness. By means of deep meditation the *atman* may be realized. The inner 'Self' is smaller than a grain of rice, yet also greater than the earth, sky and all other worlds which are encompassed by the silent, invisible, impersonal *brahman* into which the individual spirit finally merges (*Chandogya Upanisad*, 3.14,2ff). Elsewhere *brahman* is said to project the world as a spider emits its web and then withdraws it into itself (*Mundaka Upanisad*, 1.1,7).

Brahman/atman is essentially without qualities — only in its countless transitory manifestations does it appear to possess them. Its essence is Being or Reality (*sat*) where all opposites, and hence all duality, disappear, for It is the Absolute, the One transcendent essence of all forms of existence. So prestigious did this concept become that Hinduism is sometimes referred to as Brahmanism, and members of the highest caste are called brahmins from the Sanskrit word *brahmana* 'those who belong to *brahman*'.

In the oldest *Brahmanas* '*brahman*' refers to 'universal holiness' as manifested in prayer, the priesthood, and in sacrifice, a notion which led to the Upanisadic view of the one divine principle animating all nature. The essential unity of *brahman/atman* (the cosmic and psychical principle conjoined) is expressed also in the well-known Upanisadic phrase *tat tvam asi* (Thou art That).

Brahman remains the one constant factor within and beyond the ever-active life force expressed in generation, growth, decay and destruction. Every transitory individual existence (*jiva*) is merely an emanation of a minute part of *brahman/atman* and for this reason only has some value. The wise discern *brahman* in every single being, a knowledge which ensures immortality for them (*Kena Upanisad*, 2.13), and also leads to compassion for all creatures. A frequent metaphor for *brahman* is 'Ocean', denoting inexhaustible potentiality. Like *brahman* the greater part of the ocean is never visible or known, whilst the rising and disappearing waves represent the ephemeral lives of myriads of living creatures who come into existence for a while and then are reabsorbed into the Immensity (*brahman*).

According to the *Mundaka Upanisad* (1.1.4f), there are two kinds of knowledge, a higher and a lower. The former is the knowledge that *brahman* is the Imperishable source of all things; the latter includes the four Vedas, sacrificial technique, phonetics, metrics or metre, grammar, etymology and astronomy. The last six of the above constitute the six *Vedangas* 'limbs of the Veda' — works ancillary to the Veda, although sometimes regarded as part of it.

From the cosmic point of view the material world is transitory and hence ultimately unreal (*maya*). As the *Svetasvatara Upanisad* (4.10) states: 'one should know that Nature (*prakrti*) is illusion (*maya*), and that the Mighty Lord is the illusion maker. This whole world is pervaded with beings that are parts of him.' In the *Kena Upanisad* (3.15) *brahman* is called *yaksam*, an uncanny 'Something, which changes its form every moment from human shape to a blade of grass'.[12] The *maya* concept later became of great importance in the Vedanta system.

One of the main Upanisadic concepts is that of *prana*, the 'breath of life' principle, which is frequently identified with *atman*. 'Breath' not only governs respiration but all other physiological processes as well. Another concept, also common to Jainism and Buddhism, is the transmigration of spirits or souls with the associated doctrine of *karma*. This concept of conditioned rebirth henceforth dominated Indian thinking and formed the basis of new systems of thought. Even the gods are subject to *karma* and so they cannot be essentially different from man. The karmic concept also implies the eternity of the cosmic process: every existence is conditioned by a multitude of prior mental thoughts and physical acts performed either in the present existence or in countless previous existences, which allows for no definite end to the world process nor a first beginning. Everything in the world and every being is interdependent, each having its place in the scheme of things. This teaching prevents the erection of the barrier between man and animal which occurred in Judaism, Christianity and Islam, and which opened the way for the unlimited exploitation and cruelty inflicted on animals to the present day.

A person's *karma* is regarded as a power — a subtle substance that belongs to him yet which may be detached from him, as can fame, majesty, beauty and the effects of asceticism. This ancient belief derives from the notion that no thing can be represented without having an actual existence, thus every deed is conceived of as a substance. Just as the conduct of an individual is influenced by his present and previous acts, so too the collective *karmas* of all beings in the world at any time condition the type and quality of that world, and will further condition the quality of the world to follow. Some theistic cults have deified the concept of *karma* as the god Karma or Isvara who represents the collective *karma* of all creatures.

The *karma* doctrine should not be confused with the Western teaching of God's retribution since the retaliatory effects of *karma* are not decided by a deity but are immanent in all cosmic phenomena and processes, and in every deed.

Neither should the doctrine be regarded as fatalistic, for although one's present state is determined by past actions, present deeds determine one's future state.

The *karma* concept is not actually stated in the *Rgveda*, but it does mention that a person's conduct in this world determines his life after death. The *Brahmanas* stress the importance of the sacred act of sacrificing which was supposed to have a bearing on man's fate in the next world, and hence it is said that 'the sacrifice becomes the self of the sacrificer in the next world' (*Satapatha Brahmana* 11.1.8,6). The need to perform holy acts to achieve a better state in the next existence was later extended to include alms-giving and asceticism.

Karma is mentioned in one of the oldest *Upanisads*; it states that as a man lives, so he becomes. He who has done good is born again as a being having good tendencies, and he who has done evil as a being with evil tendencies, for man 'is formed entirely out of desire, and according to his desire is his resolve, and according to his resolve he performs the actions, and according to the performance of the action is his destiny' (*Brhadaranyaka Upanisad*, 4.4,28f).

The spiritual essence which passes from body to body in the series of rebirths cannot be regarded as a definite personality but is an indestructible 'Something' capable of assuming innumerable different forms. The long series of individual lives may be likened to a vast drama in which the actors assume successively different roles according to their individual *karma* coming to fruition at various times, but these different roles have no effect whatever on the individual's eternal spiritual essence.

Although the idea of world renunciation came more to the fore in the later Hindu tradition, it was foreshadowed in some of the *Upanisads*. The oldest describe *brahman/atman* as 'consisting of joy', but with the increased emphasis on the transitory nature of the world and its inhabitants, the devotee longed for the permanent bliss of mergence with *brahman* and release from the distractions and sufferings of the world. However, this state is achieved only by those few people who totally comprehend the ultimate unreality of the world and hence no longer hanker for it.

The *Maitrayana* (a post Buddhist *Upanisad*) shows a

profound distaste for the world, yet it did not lead to a paralysing nihilism or pessimism. Instead it stimulated the devotee to make every effort to master the world by means of various disciplines leading to the intuitive comprehension of the Unity (*brahman*) from which the apparent plurality of the world arises, for 'joy is the *brahman* from which all beings emerge and to which all are finally reabsorbed into joy' (*Taittiriya Upanisad*, 2.9).

All the later religio-philosophical systems are based on one or other of the *Upanisads,* and also much of the heterodox religions of Buddhism and Jainism. But when the texts of the *Upanisads* came to be regarded as divinely revealed, creative philosophical thought began to decline. Winternitz[13] points out that from the Upanisadic esoteric doctrines 'one current of thought may be traced to the mysticism of . . . Persian Sufism, to the mystic-theosophical logos doctrine of the New Platonics and the Alexandrian Christians, down to the teachings of the great German mystic of the nineteenth century, Schopenhauer.'

The works called *sutras* are manuals which deal with ritual observances, customs, law, philosophy, etc. The *Srauta Sutras* are concerned with Vedic ritual; the *Grhya-sutras* with the duties of householders; and the *Dharmasutras* with orthodox law. The *Sastras* are enlargements of the Srauta Sutras and deal with the four main aims of life for orthodox Hindus: pleasure (*kama*), economic gain (*artha*), virtue (*dharma*), and liberation (*moksa*).

A number of magical rites are included in the *Grhya Sutras,* as well as ancient customs, folk beliefs, and religious practices, many of which are common to other Indo-European peoples. For example, there are parallels in ancient Greek, Roman, Teutonic and Slavonic marriage customs with those of the *Grhya Sutras* showing 'that the relationship of the Indo-European peoples is not limited to language, but that these peoples, related in language have also preserved common features from prehistoric times in their manners and customs'.[14] The five so-called 'great sacrifices' to be performed by the head of each household are: the daily sacrifices to the gods, demons and ancestors; the fourth refers to hospitality which must be shown at all times to guests; the fifth consists in daily study of part of the Veda.

Attached to the *Srautra Sutras* are the *Sulva Sutras*, the oldest books on Indian geometry containing instructions for the measurement and construction of the complex Vedic fire altars and the laying out of the sacrificial area. There are many other texts belonging to the vast ritual literature of Hinduism which cannot be included in this brief outline.

2. The Epics

The two great Hindu Epics, the *Ramayana* and the *Mahabharata*, have profoundly affected the religious life of India. They are recited throughout the sub-continent by professional story tellers, so enabling even the illiterate to become conversant with them. Both Epics were originally secular martial ballads transmitted orally, recounting the adventures of ancient heroes and describing royal sacrificial ritual. Later the priests interpolated long passages on theology, ritual, morals, ethics and statecraft, thus making both Epics theistic.

The Ramayana

The *Ramayana* is much smaller than the *Mahabharata*. The sage Valmiki is said to be its author. According to tradition the *Ramayana* was composed about 500 BC. It received its present form two or three centuries later, but there are a number of different versions extant. The first and last of its books are the latest. The former states that Rama is an incarnation of Visnu, an indication of its later composition, but many of the stories are very old and include some which probably originated in the kingdoms of Magadha and Kosala (northern India).

The seven books of the *Ramayana* describe the adventures and vicissitudes of Rama, originally a famous tribal chief and eldest son of King Dasaratha. Rama embodies the virtues of the warrior class — great bravery, courage and fair dealing.

His wife is Sita, daughter of King Janaka. After years of married happiness Sita was captured by Ravana the demon king of Ceylon (Lanka). Rama and his half brother Laksmana searched for her, assisted by the monkey king Sugriva and the ape Hanuman. Finally Hanuman discovered Sita in Lanka and returned to India to rally his army to attack Ravana. After a tremendous battle Rama was victorious whereupon he appointed a new king. Tragically, he repudiated Sita because she had been living, albeit involuntarily, in another man's house. She threw herself on a pyre, but the fire failed to consume her because the fire-god Agni knew she was innocent. Rama and Sita were then reunited and returned to Ayodhya (the capital of the old kingdom of Kosala) where Rama was crowned king. However, the Kosalan people remained unconvinced of Sita's innocence and Rama also appears to have had doubts, for he asked Laksmana to take her far away and abandon her. This Laksmana did, but Sita found her way to Valmiki's hermitage where she gave birth to twins. When they grew up Rama recognized them as his sons. Sita then invoked the Earth to swallow her up to attest her purity. The Earth opened and received her into the depths. Shortly after, Rama abdicated in favour of his twin sons and ascended to the heavenly realms of Visnu.

The Mahabharata

The 'Great Bharata' includes the *Harivamsa* 'The Genealogy of Hari (Visnu)' and the *Bhagavadgita* 'Song of the Lord'. The *Mahabharata* is considerably larger than the *Ramayana*, and consists of over 90,000 stanzas (usually of 32 syllables). Traditionally it is attributed to Krsna Dvaipayana, also known as Vyasa the 'arranger' of the Vedas, but it is obviously the work of many hands and shows signs of much editing, interpolations and modifications. It was composed over many centuries and was almost finalized by the third or second centuries BC, although the *Bhagavadgita* and other interpolations are somewhat later. Some of the stories contain Vedic elements, which indicates its great age. The great battle described in the *Mahabharata* may have a historical basis in the memory of a battle in north India in the tenth century BC.

The *Mahabharata* provides both popular entertainment and religious instruction throughout the sub-continent. It consists of eighteen books or sections and includes many legends and customs, and much folklore. If the interpolations are omitted, the main theme is the civil war between the Kauravas and their kinsmen the Pandavas in the region of Kuruksetra (near modern Delhi); but the account of the conflict has been greatly exaggerated to take in most of India.

When King Pandu abdicated to take up the life of a hermit his sons ruled in his stead. After Pandu's death the sons of the blind Dhrtarastra, led by the eldest Duryodhana, plotted against Pandu's five sons, Yudhisthira, Bhima, Arjuna, Nakula and Sahadeva, and so harassed them that they left the country to travel from one royal court to another serving as soldiers of fortune. Finally, at the Pancala court, they met Krsna the Yadava chief who was to become their trusted friend and helper. Some years later Dhrtarastra decided to abdicate after dividing the kingdom between the Pandavas and his own sons the Kauravas, a decision which far from satisfied his sons. Then Duryodhana invited Yudhisthira to a gambling match in which Yudhisthira lost his half of the kingdom, whereupon the Pandavas and their joint wife Draupadi went into exile for thirteen years after which they were to receive their part of the kingdom back. When the thirteen years had passed the Kauravas failed to keep their promise and the Pandavas prepared for war, each side having many allies. After eighteen days of fierce fighting all the chiefs were dead except the Pandava princes and Krsna. Yudhisthira was then crowned King and he and his brothers ruled wisely and well for many years. Finally, Yudhisthira abdicated in favour of Pariksit, Arjuna's grandson. The five brothers and Draupadi then went to the Himalayas where they climbed Mount Meru and entered the realm of the gods.

The *Harivamsa* forms an appendix to the *Mahabharata* and consists of three parts which give an account of creation, a genealogical list of the Yadavas, myths, the adventures and love affairs of Krsna and the cowherd girls, and prophesies. In common with the *Mahabharata* the *Harivamsa* has been heavily revised by successive redactors, often very unskilfully. Although it purports to be part of the *Mahabharata* it is much later and in style resembles the popular works called *Puranas*.

The *Bhagavadgita* (also called the *Gita*) is included in the *Mahabharata* although it is of much later date than the Epic.

It is also later than the six orthodox philosophical systems for there is evidence that it was influenced by all of them especially by Samkhya, Yoga and Vedanta. The *Gita* represents the views of Krsna Devakiputra who declared that righteous conduct is more efficacious than gifts made to a priestly sacrificer. Thus the ancient faith in the efficacy of sacrifice as the sole means of liberation is no longer valid: only deeds springing from altruistic motives and total devotion to Isvara and faith in his grace can lead to liberation.

The *Bhagavadgita* expressly defends the ancient Indian virtues of courage, militarism and the caste system. Krsna as the Supreme Being expounds his religio-philosophical views to Arjuna, since Krsna in his human manifestation was related to the Pandavas and to the Kauravas.

The *Gita* may be interpreted in a number of ways since it includes many disparate religious views and beliefs. None the less it stresses the concept of a personal god (Isvara), also referred to as the Supreme Soul (*paramatman*) which is distinguishable from the individual soul (*atman* or *jiva*).

Before the great battle described in the *Mahabharata*, the Pandava prince Arjuna was unnerved by the thought of killing his cousins in the coming struggle. Krsna offered to act as his charioteer and adviser and pointed out that his caste duty (Arjuna was a member of the warrior caste) should take precedence over all other considerations, and that it should be carried out irrespective of the results. Krsna further pointed out that Arjuna's soul, and the souls of the Kauravas, being eternal could never be killed and would remain forever untouched by any actions done in this world. Finally Krsna revealed his true nature to Arjuna who saw the whole universe encompassed by Krsna who is also Lord of Time and hence the destroyer of worlds. Arjuna then worshipped Krsna who reminded him that it is not by sacrifices, asceticism or almsgiving that the vision of the Divine can be attained, but only by wholehearted loving devotion. Even so, he adds that any form of sincere worship performed with pure motives is acceptable to him.

In this work the divine has a twofold nature: a lower one which controls the transient world, and the higher that is the life force of all creation but which remains forever transcendent, and hence unaffected by the vicissitudes of the world. Krsna reflects this twofold nature for he is both immanent in the world as an incarnation and transcendent as the One Reality.

3. The Puranas 'Ancient Stories'

The *Puranas* are part of the auxiliary scriptural corpus of the Hindu Tradition supplementing the Veda. They consist of a vast compendia of ancient legends, religious instructions, folklore, mythology, tales of the gods, cosmogony, sacred places, rites, astrology and medical practices. Their composition is ascribed to Vyasa, the legendary author of the *Mahabharata*.

Traditionally the *Puranas* should expound five subjects (although they do not always do so): the creation of the world; its destruction and re-creation; genealogies of gods and patriarchs; reigns of the Manus of various world periods (*manvantaras*); and the history of the Solar and Lunar royal dynasties.

None of the eighteen main *Puranas* are earlier than the Gupta Period (AD 320-480), although much of the legendary material is older. The names of the eighteen *Puranas* are: Visnu, Agni, Bhavisya, Bhagavata, Naradiya, Garuda, Padma, Varaha, Matsya, Kurma, Linga, Siva, Skanda, Brahma, Brahmanda, Brahmavaivarta, Markandeya and Vamana. In some lists the Vayu is substituted for the *Agni Purana*, in others for the *Siva Purana*. The *Vayu Purana* is perhaps the oldest; some others may be as late as the fifteenth or sixteenth century, but all appear to have undergone much re-editing.

The *Puranas* greatly aided the dissemination of Upanisadic teaching to the illiterate, and to the majority of women to whom education was deliberately denied. The *Puranas* also include strong devotional (*bhakti*) elements as well as Samkhya-Yoga and Visistadvaita teachings. There are a number of subsidiary *Puranas* known as *Upapuranas*, and also many modern works of Puranic type purporting to tell of ancient times.

4. God and Gods

The Sanskrit term for god is *deva* derived from the root *div* 'to shine' or 'to be radiant'; it is applied to any abstract or cosmic potency present in any form of power which may be manifested as human beings, or as animals given divine status, or as incarnations (*avataras*). Every Indian village and district has its own local or tribal divinities as well as innumerable vegetal, forest and field godlings which, when propitiated, will both protect and bestow prosperity on the community. Certain ancient and inspired *rsis* or seers are said to have 'seen' the gods in visions.

Most of the Vedic deities are deifications of the powers of nature, with natural disasters and diseases being attributed to malevolent powers such as Vrtra, or the goddess Nirrti, the personification of decay, destruction and death. But on the whole the gods were kindly disposed towards mankind. Some of them, such as Varuna and Mitra, represent the ideal of morality, good behaviour, kindness and honesty, which indicates the high ethical standard striven for at that early time.

The composers of the *Rgveda* never ascribed supremacy to any one deity but to whichever god they were addressing in an individual hymn, other deities being regarded as subordinate. This characteristic is common to the whole of Hinduism, and a Hindu chooses a particular deity (*istadevata*) to be his Supreme Deity. One Rgvedic passage recognizes thirty-three gods (as does the Iranian tradition), but another passage states that the names of the gods are but different names for the one Supreme Being. A similar view occurs in the *Brhadaranyaka Upanisad* (3.9,1): the sage Yajnavalkya on being questioned concerning the number of gods replied, 3,306; questioned further, he replied six, three, two, one and a half, and one, and added that the last is 'the Life Breath which they call the Immensity [*brahman*]'. From the latter, universes and worlds are projected without causing any diminution of *brahman*, anymore than a dream diminishes the dreamer's unconscious. From the mundane viewpoint, *brahman* as the Supreme Deity remains linked with empirical measurement, the number 'one'; but from the transcendental point of view (the state of unchanging eternal being), *brahman* is the limitless and attributeless Absolute where all opposites are reconciled. So speculative monism has existed alongside ritualistic polytheism from Vedic times to the present day, thereby emphasizing that Reality is inexhaustible, beyond name and form, pervading and transcending all existence and earthly knowledge.

The Vedic gods were thought to rely on man's sacrificial offerings which sustained them and also kept the world process going. But neither the Vedic nor the Hindu gods are solely concerned with human welfare, for man is only a part of Nature in common with all other beings.

As classical Hinduism slowly emerged from an evolving synthesis of Aryan, Dravidian, tribal and aboriginal cults, the old Vedic gods, such as Agni, Indra, Surya and Varuna, lost much of their former importance, whilst some minor divinities like Visnu and Siva came to the fore and also assimilated many local and non-Vedic deities. But all the gods, despite their disparate origins and functions, are regarded as one or other of the countless aspects of Ultimate Reality (*brahman*). *Brahman* may be regarded as a personal deity Isvara, for those people who need a supreme, personal, loving and protecting god, or as the attributeless Absolute. Thus polytheistic elements may be subsumed under theism or under absolutism.

None of the gods created the world out of nothing. Brahma is often said to be a 'secondary' creator, creating 'new' worlds by reorganizing already existing eternal, unitary matter. Being eternal, matter is always the same yet different, and creation is likened to a potter taking a lump of clay from which he fashions many different shapes, all of them remaining, basically, mere clay.

Few Indians can accept the Hebraic-Christian doctrine that the world was created out of nothing by an external omniscient deity at a specific historical time; yet they will recognize that monotheism is but one of the many ways in which man may conceive of religious reality. The enormous variations in the characteristics of the gods of different races and cultures, and even the widely differing beliefs in one society, are explained by the multiplicity of man's views of God. The very differences indicate the relative nature of all deities. Thus to the Indian mind pantheism, polytheism, monotheism and monism are all equally valid paths to the Divine. Even atheistic views are included in the Hindu Tradition as can be seen in the early teachings of Samkhya and the materialist Carvakas who were active from before the sixth century BC until the medieval period, when they lost most of their following.

By the first century AD most educated Hindus were either Vaisnavas or Saivas. They lived amicably side by side, with no feeling of exclusiveness among the members of these cults, since a Vaisnava does not deny the existence of Siva and *vice versa;* each god is regarded by his devotees as an aspect of the one indefinable *brahman.* Such mutual tolerance led naturally to syncretistic divine forms such as the triad (*trimurti*) promulgated in Gupta times. It consists of Brahma (the 'secondary' creator), Visnu the preserver of the world, and Siva. Although each of these deities is associated with a specific cosmic function, they are essentially three manifestations of the one Supreme Being.

Visnu, like the Christian God, incarnates himself to save mankind; but Visnu incarnates himself a number of times for the same purpose when the world becomes very evil, and assumes different forms appropriate to the circumstances. This notion of a loving god devoted to the welfare of mankind invariably has a strong appeal. Visnu's avatars are but minute particles of the supramundane essence of godhead. Siva is the third member of the triad. His special function is to preside over the dissolution of the world; but he too can intervene to save it when it is endangered before the long cosmic cycle is due to end, as he did when he swallowed the poison that otherwise would have destroyed all life on earth. A more popular syncretism than the triad was that of Harihara (Hari is a name for Visnu, and Hara is a name of Siva). This cult enabled the worshipper to apprehend the two deities simultaneously.

Although the Vedic gods lost their supremacy they never disappeared completely, since Hindus never suppress any divinity or belief but merely add new ones. As all beings are expressions of the eternal divine essence, they are essentially non-different from one another. Thus famous heroes like Krsna and the three Ramas achieved divine status as incarnations of Visnu.

Sometimes the gods may be depicted in animal form or as half-man and half-animal, as in ancient Egypt, Greece, Babylonia and elsewhere. Some of these forms may stem from much earlier cults assimilated to the cults of the major deities but, apart from these, particular animals and birds were chosen because they convey so forcibly ideas of fertility, virility, speed, beauty, or spirituality. The bull for example expresses virility, fertility and power; the stallion speed, fecundity and beauty; the elephant enormous strength, longevity and wisdom; and the high-flying snow-white goose suggests total freedom, as it is at home on water, earth and in the air, as well as symbolizing purity and man's striving for the Divine. Snakes (*nagas*) are both feared and venerated and serpent shrines are found in many parts of India; these reptiles know the location of the mineral treasures of the earth, and guard them. Serpent cults have penetrated into most of the world's religions, including Jainism, Buddhism and Hinduism, as well as remaining a popular cult among villagers and farmers. The Indian mind sees nothing strange in using animal forms to symbolize particular abstract ideas, since everything in the world is in essence divine. Every single world, creature, plant or stone is a manifestation of the mysterious forces of nature, and hence gods may be manifested in any form for all nature is *in* God (*brahman*).

According to some of the Vedantic schools, God's nature consists of 'being', 'consciousness' and 'bliss' (*sac-cid-ananda*). In the Advaita Vedanta system God is regarded as a 'lower' manifestation of *brahman*, the Absolute *brahman* being without attributes or qualities.

Each deity has a consort: Brahma's is the lovely goddess of creative intelligence, Sarasvati; Visnu's, the goddess of good fortune and beauty, Laksmi; and Siva's, the mountain goddess Parvati. All these goddesses are divine representations of the essential creative powers of divinity.

In the widespread devotional theistic cults, worship consists of loving adoration of, and complete devotion to, the worshipper's chosen deity. One who truly loves God becomes immersed in his own intrinsic bliss and therefore desires nothing else. Such intense devotion actually transforms the worshipper's personality and is not merely a temporary emotional state. The Supreme Being is not represented as a jealous and exclusive god as in the Semitic religions, but as one who understands every kind of worshipper and every kind of belief. The Supreme Being is perfect love himself and he welcomes all devotees of whatever understanding or spiritual level, or of whatever faith, yet at the same time he is supremely detached — being totally free of egoism. Thus in the *Bhagavadgita* (7,21ff) Krsna (the main incarnation of Visnu) is made to say: 'Whatever devotee seeks to worship, whatsoever divine form with fervent faith, I, verily, make that faith of his unwavering'. In the same work Krsna states that he is the taste in water, the brilliance of fire, the life in all beings, the majesty of the majestic, the courage of the courageous, the knowledge of the learned, and so on. Although God (Krsna) is the animating principle in everything, this theism differs from pantheism in that God is regarded as more than the universe: 'Whatever creature possesses lordliness or majesty or greatness, know that every such creature springs from a fraction of My Glory . . . With *one part* of Myself I remain the support of this entire universe.'

The great diversity of man's spiritual conceptions is explained by the Samkhya teaching of the three *gunas,* the main constituents comprising everything in the world. Thus in the highest conception of divinity as the embodiment of goodness, beneficence, perfection, and radiance, the *sattva guna* predominates; when god is regarded as wrathful, cruel and violent, the *rajas guna* is uppermost; and when a god of disease, pestilence, destruction and death is envisaged the *tamas guna* is to the fore. From this it follows that the nature, characteristics and personality attributed to a deity depend largely on the predominating *guna* in the character of the devotee, and any quality attributed to a god is merely the reflection of the worshipper's own mental state, inclinations, tendencies, and level of spirituality, but *not* of Reality. Furthermore, the application of human terms and concepts to deity, like lord, saviour, or protector, fails to express the immensity of Divine reality of which man can only comprehend the merest fragment. The Ultimate Reality is an unknown 'Something' far beyond the confines of human personality and man's need for protection, support and happiness. None the less all genuine attempts to approach the Divine are legitimate for some see the many in the One, others the One in the many, but essentially the Divine is 'the All'.

The Years of the Gods

The final system of Hindu cosmology indicates a synthesis, which took place over many centuries, of some originally independent doctrines; and this gave rise to a number of inconsistencies.

According to Hindu cosmology, a beginningless series of worlds pass through cycles within cycles forever. One 'day of Brahma' consists of 4,320 million earthly years and is called a *kalpa;* his 'night' is of equal length; his 'year' contains 360 such days and nights; and his lifetime is 100 divine years, that is 311,040,000 million years. At the end of this vast period the universe dissolves into non-manifestation, until aeons later another 'secondary' creator-god appears and a 'new' world unfolds. During his 'day' Brahma creates the universe from eternally existing matter and finally absorbs it, where it remains latent during the 'night' of Brahma, after which the process starts again.

Each *kalpa* is divided into fourteen secondary cycles (*manvantaras*), each lasting millions of years and with vast intervals between the cycles. During these periods another world comes into being and a new Manu appears as the progenitor of the human race. At present we are in the seventh *manvantara* whose Manu is Vaivasvata.

Each *manvantara* comprises seventy-one aeons called *mahayugas*, each divided into four ages (*yugas*), called *krta, treta, dvapara* and *kali,* and consisting of 4,800; 3,600; 2,400;

and 1,200 'years of the gods' respectively. (A 'year of the gods' consists of 360 human years.) The above ages are sometimes named after metals — gold, silver, copper and iron, respectively. We are now in the *kali* age when goodness, kindness, virtue, justice, strength, longevity and happiness are at their lowest ebb. The present age commenced in 3102 BC which is also the traditional date of the *Mahabharata* war. Each successive world develops like a living organism and hence its vitality weakens over thousands of years until it disintegrates to give place to the next, according to the law of cosmic cycles. In all these worlds the eternal *dharma* (the order governing every manifestation of the cosmos) remains always the same. Morality and goodness also weaken in the succeeding periods. In the golden age all beings observed *dharma*, three-quarters in the silver age, half in the copper or bronze age, and only a quarter in the present debased age. There is no beginning or end to the indefinite succession of universes, a concept symbolized by a wheel. Its outer rim forever circles round its eternal unchanging axis — *brahman*.

5. The Goddess (Devi) and Others

The widespread worship of the non-Aryan Mother Goddess stretches back to the Neolithic past and is common to most ancient cultures. It is based on the observance of the human mother who brings forth new life from her womb and nourishes, cherishes and protects the infant from all dangers. This mother-child relationship appeals to many worshippers more than the more distant father-child relationship. But the patriarchal-based religion of the Aryans drove worship of the Mother Goddess underground — to reappear centuries later as powerful as ever. She was probably worshipped by the people of the Indus Valley civilization as the female figurines found there would suggest. Many of the pre-Aryan goddesses of the indigenes were later assimilated into Hinduism as manifestations of the multi-named Mother Goddess of the Vedas.

The Rgvedic goddesses are regarded as wives of the gods, or as personifications of religious worship such as Ida, who represents the sacrificial food or libations, and Hotra and Svaha, personifications of the ritual invocations. Similarly Night (Ratri) is personified as a goddess, as are a number of rivers including the Ganga (Ganges), Yamuna, and Sarasvati. Although the *Rgveda* implies that the goddesses are subordinate to the gods, Aditi none the less stands out from the rest. She represents freedom and infinity that contains everything else including the gods. In one aspect she is the

Great Mother identified with the Cosmic Cow (the symbol of motherhood and the overflowing abundance of nature). She is invoked to give freedom from all kinds of harm. Her twelve sons, collectively called the Adityas, represent the months of the solar year and are invoked to bestow benefits on mankind. Another goddess to whom about twenty fine hymns are addressed is Usas, the rosy goddess of the dawn, who signifies the victory of light over darkness and life over death.

Other Vedic goddesses include Prthivi the 'Broad', the personification of the Earth; Diti, the mother of the Daityas, who were originally native tribes opposed to the Vedic religion (in later mythology regarded as demons); Aranyani, the elusive goddess of forests and wild creatures; Vac (Speech); Puramdhi and Dhisana, both representing abundance; Raka and Sinivali, beneficent goddesses who later became the presiding deities of the full and new moon respectively; Ila the 'mother of the cattle herds'; Asuniti, the personification of the 'world of spirits' invoked to bestow strength and longevity; and Nirrti, goddess of misfortune, decay and death.

Most Vedic goddesses represent the ever-productive forces of nature whereas the non-Vedic predominantly symbolize fertility. Both concepts became inextricably intermingled in the symbolism of the Goddess who represents generation and the glories of life with the ever-present process of disintegration and death. Therefore she has two aspects: one compassionate, gentle and loving; the other fierce, cruel, violent and dark with destruction. Yet even in her fierce aspect, she protects those of her devotees who can overcome their fears of the terrors of the inevitable process of continuous change and decay she represents, to see also her transcendent beauty and the eternal bliss that ultimately she bestows on her worshippers.

In the Sakta and Tantric cults the goddess, as Sakti, represents the visible universe arising from the universal, inaccessible, motionless substratum *brahman*. In other words, the ultimate principle of the universe is regarded as female. Sakti is the overflowing cosmic energy through which gods, worlds and all creatures come into being. In fact, she is indistinguishable from Nature (*prakrti*).

The goddess has many names resulting from her assimilation of local and tribal divinities, some of a particularly bloodthirsty nature. In post-Vedic times Sakti is conceived as the power (*sakti*) of the gods and is associated with them as their consorts. Literary references to her become more frequent from the seventh century onwards when she became Siva's consort. Her gentle forms are called Parvati, Uma, Padma and Gauri; her fierce forms, Syama, Bhairavi, Camunda, Kali and Durga, and they are often depicted as garlanded with skulls. As Durga, she destroys the demon Mahisa and pursues evil everywhere; as Camunda and Kali she represents the power of death, famine and disease; as the Seventh of Eight Mothers she personifies the energies of the chief gods. This two-fold aspect signifies the continuous struggle between life and death, good and evil. The emphasis on both sides of the life process enables the more spiritually advanced devotees to understand, accept and no longer fear the vicissitudes of life which none can escape. As a goddess in her own right she is Devi, the form of the Immensity (*brahman*) from which the world arises as Nature and Person (*prakrti-purusa*). Some Sakta works identify Sakti with the exquisitely beautiful goddess Tripurasundari, embodiment of the bliss aspect of the formless *brahman* (*nirguna brahman*).

The ugly, emaciated, skull-garlanded goddess Kali is especially popular in Bengal, where her cult has somewhat overshadowed many of the local deities such as Manasa, the goddess of snakes, Sitala, goddess of smallpox, Candi, goddess of hunters, and others. Kali also includes among her many manifestations: the ten Mahavidyas, personifications of her supernatural knowledge; the Seven Mothers (Saptamatrikas), identified with the seven Sanskrit vowels (five pure and two mixed e, o), which form the basis of all language and hence represent the power of language, which is regarded as an independent entity; the sixty-four Yoginis, incarnations of the forces of yoga and of shamanic magic; and the Dakinis, malignant spirits who eat raw flesh and are attendant on Durga.

The goddess Sakti is one of the three divinities who emerged from the amalgamation of a number of disparate traditions and cultural complexes which grew up over the centuries. The other two are Visnu/Krsna and Siva. One or other of them is worshipped by their sectarian followers as the Supreme Being. Non-sectarian Hindus also recognize these divinities and others, as representatives of different facets of the Divine.

Today the most popular goddess is Sri, the personification of prosperity and beauty. She is mentioned once in the *Rgveda* and more frequently in the *Atharvaveda* and other works. Later she became linked with the post-Vedic goddess Laksmi, who emerged from the Ocean of Milk (representing abundance *in potentia*) when the gods and *asuras* churned it. The association of the two goddesses and the varied myths associated with them suggests the assimilation of numerous folk traditions. Sri is said to dwell in garlands and hence prosperity, good fortune and victory are ensured to those who wear them. She is also closely connected with goodness and with the soil: after her death a rice plant grew from her navel; and her fertility aspect is shown by her association with dung (hence her epithet *Karisin*, 'abounding in dung').

6. Spirits, Sprites and Godlings

Alongside the ancient Vedic cult and the present-day Vaisnava, Saiva and Sakta cults, countless forms of animism, nature worship and demonology exist in India. Every river, mountain, forest or field has its presiding deity, as do houses, temples, shrines, roads, paths and villages. Most of these local spirits stem from the ancient aboriginal past and many have been absorbed gradually by the higher cults. These spirits may be worshipped in groves, on hills, outside settlements or under sacred trees.

The mysterious beings called Yaksas (also common to Buddhism and Jainism) are apparitions or manifestations of the numinous. They frequent lonely places and were probably the vegetal godlings of pre-Aryan communities. Yaksas are often honoured by a stone tablet or altar placed under a sacred village tree, their presence ensuring the prosperity of the village. Their feminine counterparts, the Yaksis, symbolize the life sap of vegetation. Some Yaksas cause insanity and other diseases. Thus a person suffering from hydrophobia was bathed at a cross roads accompanied by a prayer: 'O thou Yaksa, who are the lord of dogs, free me from the poison of the rabid dog that has bitten me' (*Susruta Samhita*, II. p. 736).

In common with other supernatural beings, Yaksas may be benevolent or malevolent towards man. As protectors of the community they are often depicted on local shrines and doorposts as handsome, virile, powerful men. Coomaraswamy considers it probable that the later cult images of Siva, the Yoginis, the Seven Mothers, and some forms of the goddess Devi, were modelled on Yaksa forms. In later mythology the leader of the Yaksas is Kubera, god of wealth.

Included among the multitude of spirits are the Pretas, ethereal forms of the newly dead. Those long dead become ancestors or Fathers (*Pitrs*), yet both Pretas and Pitrs remain active in the world and occasionally assist their descendants, as in the case of the fainting Bhisma when they appeared as 'soul' birds to support him. The deceased cannot be united with his ancestors and raised to the status of a Pitr until the correct funerary rites (*sraddhas*) have been performed, rites which include the offering of water and funerary cakes (*pindas*) to the three immediate generations of the deceased's forebears. The offerings provide nourishment for their ethereal bodies as well as gaining merit for the donors. The Pitrs are highly revered and called the 'divinities of the gods'. Their realm is sometimes identified with heaven (*svarga*), but more often is conceived of as a nether world situated in the South and identified with Yamaloka — the realm of the judge of the dead, Yama.

The souls of those who die violent deaths become malevolent Bhutas (night-wandering ghosts) who are assimilated to particular Pretas, especially those who have died unnatural deaths or whose funerary rites have not been performed. Bhutas haunt trees and derelict buildings and are worshipped by some low caste people in northern India, who also incorporate them in their magical practices. In modern India they are regarded as the spirits of the dead, being completely merged with Pretas.

Troops of Bhutas are said to follow armies, but not all are malevolent for some praise and laud great heroes. Pretas, and other demonic spirits called Pisacas, also appear dancing among the dead and wounded on battlefields, or in burial grounds. They personify the forces of darkness, cruelty, violence and death as do the Yatudhanas, guardians of Kubera's mountain. The Yatudhanas are associated with the aboriginal tribes and are said to have animal hoofs like the medieval Christian Devil. They are mentioned in the *Rgveda* where Agni is invoked to burn up female fiends (Yatudhanis), and more frequently in the *Atharavaveda* where the *apamarga* plant is said to nullify their curses and spells. The *Mahabharata* attributes all kinds of calamities to them, especially the ailments of women and children.

Among the other spirits are Raksasas, Bhairavas, Nagas, Asuras and Vetalas. Both Raksasas and Pisacas are hideous, bloodthirsty, nocturnal eaters of raw flesh. From twilight onwards through the night their powers increase. Pisacas may 'possess' people, but the *Atharvaveda* provides protection against them by means of mantras and specific plants. Pisacas can assume any shape, or remain invisible, and so can easily enter a person's mouth when yawning. They frequent cremation sites looking for unburnt corpses to inhabit and so terrify the living. Bhairavas are the terror-inspiring attendants of Rudra (or are sometimes regarded as aspects of Siva). Nagas are serpent deities and guardians of the treasures of the earth. Asuras are skilled in magic and powerful in battle. In the *Rgveda* Asura is synonymous with 'god' (*deva*), as is apparent in the invocation to Varuna as the Great Asura, and when Rudra is called the 'Asura of mighty heaven'; but from the later Vedic period onwards the term is applied to demons. A demoness, Asuri, is mentioned in the *Atharvaveda*, who produced a remedy for leprosy. Vetalas resemble vampires who reanimate the dead. Their eerie singing, like that of Bhutas and other spirits, is often heard in cemeteries. Vetala is also a term for a kind of black magic.

Other beings belonging to the sphere between man and gods are the Gandharvas, celestial musicians and inspirers of earthly musicians, singers and dancers. Their female counterparts, the nymph-like Apsarases, the dancers of the gods, may cause the madness of passion, gambling, and war in men. Both Gandharvas and Apsarases dwell in specific trees such as the *asvattha* from which their cymbals and lutes may be heard. They are besought to bestow their favours on wedding processions and to give luck to dice players. The Asparases are so exquisitely beautiful that the gods sometimes send them to seduce ascetics whose powers are becoming too great. The nymphs are said to choose their lovers from among the dead on battlefields and to carry them to Indra's paradise, a role similar to that of the Germanic Valkyries.

The Yoginis (the female form of Yogi) are regarded as witches or demonesses, which reflects the misogynist attitude of much of the Indian tradition, and also explains the ban on women attempting to practise yoga — for which they will be condemned to hell. The Yoginis are attendant on Durga and Siva, and are sometimes regarded as minor epiphanies of Durga. They incarnate the forces of shamanic magic as well as yoga. Other demonesses associated with Durga are the Sakinis and Dakinis, eaters of raw flesh. The Dakinis are connected with both Buddhist and Hindu Tantrism.

This great variety of spiritual beings meets the differing requirements of people whose upbringing, intelligence and level of spirituality varies from individual to individual. Even in high civilizations advanced and archaic beliefs exist simultaneously. The most spiritually advanced persons are said to worship the impersonal *brahman;* those who incline towards action worship Yaksas and Asuras; and those who desire excitement worship ghosts. This notion is based on the concept of the three *gunas,* which forms the basis of the different types of personality.

7. The Six Orthodox Philosophical Systems

The Sanskrit term for philosophy is *darsana*, from *drsti*, literally a 'seeing', 'vision of truth', or 'viewpoint'. Behind the main Hindu philosophical systems lies a vast and complex development spread over nearly 2,000 years, which can be treated in this work only very briefly and in much simplified form.

Although Indian philosophy is inextricably bound up with religious beliefs and the attainment of liberation, it is still possible for an orthodox Hindu to be an atheist. Some of the traditional systems are also atheistic in so far as they deny the existence of a creator god. But Indian atheism is not necessarily anti-religious as is the atheism of the West, for the Indian atheist may pray to a god or gods who are regarded as *part* of the universe, not external to it. He may also accept the doctrine of rebirth yet not accept that a single deity, at a specific moment, created the world from nothing. Most Hindu thinkers, despite their diverse views, accept some fundamental presuppositions such as *karma*, rebirth, liberation and the Unity underlying apparent multiplicity. They also accept the concept of the successive unfurling of worlds and universes and their disintegration. Our earth is but a tiny speck in the incomprehensible vastness of space, and human life the merest ripple in the ocean of cosmic time. During the recurring cosmic cycles, civilizations rise and fall; species appear and disappear; great nations arise and pass away;

religions appear, flourish for a time and then fade away; periods of barbarism and war alternate with periods of prosperity and peace. This broad view enables the Indian thinker to take a more detached view of life and to realize the relative insignificance and transitory nature of all things and beings; he ceases to cling to that which is fleeting and instead strives to reach Ultimate Reality for although man's body is limited in space and time, his soul or spirit is eternal.

It was customary for philosophers to take part in regular public debates with members of other schools and hence none of the main systems developed in isolation. Such openness of mind and willingness to learn from others accounts for the tolerant attitude towards the viewpoints of others, and for the well-formulated and highly sophisticated tenets of much of Indian philosophy. Although these systems did not all arise at the same time, they existed amicably together for centuries and their followers may be found in India today.

In the centuries following the rise of the Buddha and the Jaina Mahavira, six orthodox (*astika*) religio-philosophical systems developed. They all accepted the authority of the Vedas, although their interpretations varied on other points, and include theistic, monistic, atheistic and dualistic views. But not one of these systems ever attained the status of an exclusive, dogmatic orthodoxy, for the orthodoxy of Hinduism has never been based on any one central teaching or organization. Despite their differences, these systems are regarded as complementary aspects or views of the one truth seen from differing points of view. In fact, the contradictions are more apparent than real and serve to show the limiting nature of any single method of approach.

Nothing is known of the actual or supposed founders of these schools and their names are probably those of the schools rather than of individuals. Each school has a specific *Sutra* attributed to the supposed founder. Without commentaries these works are often obscure, being intended initially as short mnemonic 'aids' for teachers who taught their pupils orally.

The six systems are usually coupled in pairs: Samkhya (based on intellectual knowledge) and Yoga (on control of the senses and inner faculties); the Vaisesika (the experimental point of view based on sensorial experience), the Nyaya (logical view based on dialectics); Vedanta (based on metaphysical speculation), and Mimamsa (deistic and ritualistic point of view based on the sacred texts). The second system of each pair is more a methodology, than a metaphysical school. Thus a follower of Yoga uses Samkhya metaphysics as the philosophy behind the practice of classical Yoga. However, the traditional scheme of six philosophies is largely artificial because in Vedanta there are important differences in interpretation, giving rise to a number of Vedantic schools. There are also other systems such as the Saiva Siddhanta lying outside the traditional six systems.

The three main unorthodox systems (*nastika*) are the Buddhist, Jaina and Carvaka. The first two deny the authority of the Vedas but believe in some kind of future life; the materialist Carvakas deny both propositions.

Samkhya

The literal meaning of Samkhya is 'enumeration'. It is a system of dualistic realism attributed to the semi-mythical sage Kapila and closely associated with the Yoga system. Yoga serves as a practical technique of liberation, the Samkhya providing the metaphysical background, although there are also minor differences between the two systems.

The oldest extant Samkhya text is the *Samkhyakarika* of Isvara-Krsna (third or fourth century AD). The basic ideas of both Samkhya and Yoga are immensely old and stem from an aboriginal non-Vedic Indian past. They were later included in the orthodox systems of the Hindu Tradition after Samkhya-Yoga adherents accepted the authority of the Vedas.

Two ultimate eternal realities are recognized in this system, Spirit (*purusa*) and Nature (*prakrti*). *Prakrti* is a single all-pervasive, unconscious, complex substance which evolves in the world into countless different shapes. This unitary, ever-changing substance cannot be seen but only inferred. Its three main constituents or elements are the *gunas: sattva, rajas* and *tamas.* Each *guna* has distinct characteristics, which to some extent are antagonistic to the others, yet they always coexist, cohere, and cooperate to produce everything in the world. The *sattva guna* consists of essence, brightness, goodness and truth; *rajas,* of force, energy, action and passions; and *tamas,* of darkness, mass, inertia and ignorance. Everything may be classified as good, bad or indifferent, or as intelligent, active or indolent, according to whichever *guna* predominates.

When the three *gunas* are in a state of equilibrium, manifestation cannot occur. The unfolding of a new world commences only when *purusa* and *prakrti* (the causeless first cause) associate (*samyoga*) whereupon *prakrti* begins the long process of differentiation. The mere presence of *purusa* is said to be sufficient to activate *prakrti*, although *purusa* itself remains unmoved.

Purusa is non-matter or 'pure spirit' which can be described only in negative terms; it is without qualities, attributes or parts and is imperishable. Viewed from the cosmic aspect, *prakrti* is the mysterious, tremendous power which unfolds and dissolves worlds over countless aeons; from the psychological aspect it is present in individual beings as the intellect (*buddhi*) an evolution of matter. *Prakrti* is therefore the source of the twenty-three principles (*tattvas*) or categories that make up the world. The eternal *purusa* (the twenty-fourth category) does not arise from *prakrti* (the twenty-fifth category) because both are eternal. Such a concept does not require a creator god since *prakrti* is the adequate cause of the world process and hence initially the Samkhya system was atheistic. However under the influence of the Yoga system with which it later coalesced, it became theistic and a twenty-sixth category was added — called Isvara (Lord or God).

Basically there is only One *purusa*, but when manifestation occurs it is broken up, as it were, into a multitude of souls or spirits. Some of these spirits are liberated; others are still bound to individual bodies embedded in nature and are undergoing the long series of rebirths and redeaths, sometimes incarnated in human, animal or in other forms of life. Although in essence the Spirit is always free, it can be liberated from its entanglement with matter only through knowledge, virtuous living, and the practice of Yoga. It is the lack of knowledge of the fundamental distinction (*viveka*) between Self and non-Self that is responsible for all our sorrows and sufferings which are rooted in material existence. To experience this separation requires long, hard, spiritual training with constant meditation on the truth that the pure eternal consciousness is beyond the mind/body complex and beyond the 'cause and effect' order of mundane existence.

When liberation is attained the individual Self ceases to be affected by life's vicissitudes, and observes dispassionately the passing events of the world without being repelled, attracted, or implicated in them. Liberation may be attained either in this life (*jivanmukti*) or in the next world (*videhamukti*). When finally released from the psycho-physical organism (including the intellect) the spirit remains eternally unconscious, since the material basis essential for all psychical processes is missing. A temporary release occurs in deep dreamless sleep and in fainting fits.

Yoga

Yoga is a theistic system having many similarities to Samkhya. It accepts most of Samkhya epistemology, including the twenty-five principles (but adds one more, Isvara or God), and also the view that individual souls emerge from the Universal Soul and are as many as the bodies in which they incarnate. Yoga applies Samkhya teaching to everyday life, as the *Svetasvatara Upanisad* (6,13) states: 'Samkhya is knowledge, Yoga is practice.'

The *Yoga Sutras* are attributed to Patanjali, of whom little is known. The first of the books of Sutras may date from the second century BC.

The eight steps of yogic practice are:

1. Restraint (*yama*), abstention from causing physical or mental pain to any living creature; the avoidance of mental and physical unchastity, lying, stealing and greed, since desire for possessions and for new experiences distracts the mind and dissipates one's energy.
2. Discipline (*niyama*), involving the cultivation of moral virtues including kindness, friendliness, contentment, indifference to the imperfections of others, constant study of the Vedas and other sacred texts, and praising and repeating the name of one's chosen divinity. As everything is understood through a sequence of 'spoken sounds' it follows that, 'by constant practice of the rhythmic repetition of certain basic syllables while meditating on their meaning, we are able to rouse and capture the energy latent in them; we can thereby gain knowledge of all that is expressed through sounds, all the sciences of this and other words'.[1]

3. The adoption of a comfortable position (*asana*), the most usual being the *padmasana*, the cross-legged position in which the Buddha and most Hindu deities are depicted.
4. The technique of breath control (*pranayama*), which should be taught by an expert.
5. Withdrawal of the senses (*pratyahara*) from external stimuli.
6. Concentration (*dharana*) on a specific object of contemplation.
7. Uninterrupted one-pointed meditation (*dhyana*) on a particular object.
8. Total absorption (*samadhi*) on fire, or God, or a specific object until the individual consciousness merges completely in the object and is no longer aware of itself. In other words there is no dualism, no consciousness of self and not-self once the spontaneous activities of mind have ceased. As the *Yogasutras* (3,51) state: 'When the purity of contemplation equals the purity of the life-monad (*purusa*), that is isolation.'

In Yoga philosophy the Supreme Being is eternal, all-pervading and omniscient, able to bring about the association of the eternal divine principles of *prakrti* (matter or nature, later regarded as feminine) and *purusa* (Cosmic Being or Spirit, eternal and unchanging, regarded as male) which results in the unfolding of the cosmic process. The same Being also brings about the dissolution of the world by the separation of *prakrti* and *purusa*. Because nature was regarded as feminine and spirit as masculine, the deities Siva and Sakti were easily assimilated to this concept as were other divine pairs associated with Tantric cults.

According to Yoga the individual Self or Spirit is in essence pure consciousness, free from all bodily and mental limitations, but through ignorance it confuses itself with the mind and body. This is because the spirit reflects the changing states and processes of the mind and 'appears to be subject to changes and to pass through different states of the mind . . . in the same way in which the moon appears to be moving when we see it reflected in the moving waves'.[2]

The ultimate aim of Yoga and of Samkhya is the cessation of all mental modifications, *not* contact or mergence with God or *brahman*. The individual spirit must liberate itself from the grip of matter by vigorous efforts and self-discipline to the final state of perfect isolation (*kaivalya*), free from material contact, from suffering and from communion with other liberated spirits. None the less, devotion to God is part of the practice of Yoga and is believed by many to be the best means for the attainment of concentration, mind control, and the purification of consciousness which prepare the way for liberation. God is the ideal object of meditation. By his grace he removes the evils and impurities of the yogin's life, a notion that appears to cut across the doctrine of *karma*, but God's grace is said to be withheld if the devotee is unworthy of it.

For centuries Yoga has taught what Western philosophy has discovered only recently — that there are many more levels of consciousness than is generally realized, and that only when these levels are actually *experienced* can man achieve his full physical and psychical potential.

Vaisesika

Initially this was an atheistic system attributed to the legendary sage Kanada (also known as Uluka) and based on the *Vaisesikasutra* (c. AD 100).

The early Vaisesika promulgated an atomistic account of the universe somewhat similar to Buddhist, Jaina and Ajivika viewpoints. It was based on the concept that everything in the world (except soul, the substratum of consciousness, time, space and mind) is composed of various combinations of atoms — uncreated, invisible, eternal entities, which remain after a material object has been reduced to its smallest part. Although atoms are devoid of qualities, they possess potentialities that are realized only when the soul is in union with the organ of thought (*manas*), whereupon its faculties become capable of activity. In other words, separate individual atoms have no extension until combined with others when they become extensive and visible as substances. Thus during the periods of world dissolution the atoms are no longer combined and hence the visible world dissolves. This long cosmic night of dissolution is necessary for the refreshment of souls exhausted by their continuous activities. During the interim period their good and bad *karma* remain latent until the process begins again.

When the Vaisesika merged with the Nyaya system it became theistic through the introduction of the concept of God, or Supreme Soul (*paramatman*), to 'explain' how the world and everything in it arises from different combinations of eternal atoms. God is therefore a 'secondary' Creator, periodically creating worlds from eternally existent matter.

Nyaya

This is a system of logical realism founded by the sage Gotama — also known as Gautama and by his nickname Aksapada. It is based on the *Nyayasutra* which was probably composed about the second century AD, although containing much earlier material.

In common with all other Indian systems it is a philosophy meant for living. For the attainment of true knowledge necessitates an understanding and analysis of what knowledge is, its sources, the validity of its arguments and the methods for distinguishing false from true knowledge.

There are five members or clauses in the system of the Nyaya philosophy:

1. the proposition, e.g. there is a fire on the mountain.
2. the cause, for the mountain smokes.
3. the exemplification, wherever there is smoke there is fire.
4. the recapitulation of the cause, the mountain smokes, and
5. the conclusion, therefore there is fire on the mountain.

Nyaya teaching states that the existence of ideas, beliefs, visions, and emotions are all dependent on a mind, since without a mind to 'think them' they would not exist. However, such things as animals, plants, rivers, mountains, houses, monuments, etc., not being dependent on our minds, exist whether or not we know or 'think them'. The body is composed of matter, the mind (*manas*) of a subtle, indivisible, eternal substance (*anu*); but the Self (*atman*) is distinct from both. It acquires consciousness only when related to an object through the senses. Thus, since consciousness is an *added* and not an essential quality of the Self, it ceases to qualify the Self when liberation is attained. In other words, liberation consists in the realization that the Self is distinct from the body, mind, senses, etc., thereby freeing the Self from all desires and attachments transmitted to the mind by the senses. Henceforth all actions are performed altruistically (so preventing the accumulation of new *karma*) culminating in the absolute cessation of all pain and suffering, for the soul without consciousness exists as a pure substance.

There is no mention of God in the *Nyayasutra* because souls and matter are both eternal and uncreated, the destiny of an individual being in accordance with his or her *karma*. However, later, when the Vaisesika merged with the Nyaya about the ninth century or earlier (and perhaps with some Saivite influence), the Nyaya became theistic. God is said to have created the world and its inhabitants out of eternally existing atoms, that individual souls may undergo experiences in accordance with their *karma*; but sooner or later all individuals will attain liberation by means of right knowledge of themselves and of the world — whereupon the liberated Soul, devoid of consciousness, will exist as pure substance. The complete isolation of the Spirit in this system is the same as the Samkhya view of liberation.

The Nyaya-Vaisesika regards God as a distinct Soul, differing from other souls in that God is omniscient and omnipotent and thereby qualified to rule the universe; another difference is that he has never been entangled in the series of existences undergone by other souls. A number of 'proofs' were put forward for the existence of God, including those used in the West for the same purpose.

For some years the adherents of the Nyaya were in conflict with the Buddhists, until the sixth century when Uddyotakara remodelled its doctrines and incorporated many of the Mahayana Buddhist logical teachings of Dignaga. Then, during the thirteenth century, a new and highly sophisticated school of logic, the Navyanyaya ('new logic'), was developed by the Nyaya-Vaisesika.

Vedanta, including Advaita, Visistadvaita, Dvaita, and Visuddhadvaita Vedanta

The term Vedanta means 'the end of the Veda', the culmination of Vedic speculation. The basic text is the *Brahmasutra* or *Vedanta-sutra* attributed to Badarayana and composed sometime between AD 200 and 450. It comprises over five hundred short ambiguous verses open to diverse interpretations and hence necessitates the use of commentaries, the most notable being those by Sankara, Ramanuja, Madhva and Bhatrhari.. The last postulated the concept of Sabdhabrahman, that is, that the essence of *brahman* is sound or word. As all objects are manifestations of their names, ultimately they must be identical with *brahman*, the source of naming.

Vedanta is not limited to one school but subsumes within itself a number of groups. They hold differing viewpoints concerning the nature of *brahman* as expounded in the *Upanisads*, which include doctrines of pure monism (*advaita*), and modified dualism (*dvaita*), etc. Traditional Vedanta consists of the 'later exegesis' of the Veda called *uttaramimamsa* coupled with the 'earlier exegesis', *purvamimamsa*. The main schools within Vedanta are: Advaita (non-dualism), Visistadvaita (qualified non-dualism), and Dvaita (dualism). They differ radically on specific issues, such as the relation of the Self with ultimate reality (*brahman*), although each system has the same subject matter.

The first systematizers were Gaudapada and Sankara (eighth century) who established the non-dualistic system known as Advaita Vedanta. It includes many features adopted from Mahayana Buddhism, especially the doctrine of *sunyavada* which stresses the relativity and impermanency, and hence emptiness, of every concept. Guadapada's main doctrine was that there cannot be any origination because only *brahman* is real. The world and its inhabitants are merely an appearance, conjured up by the play (*lila*) of the Divine, and having no more substantiality than a dream. Sankara based his doctrine on the famous passage 'thou art That' (*tat tvam asi*) of the *Chandogya Upanisad* (6.10,3). 'Thou' and 'that' are not subject and object but are identical without difference (*a-bheda*) like the real Self (*atman*). In other words the Self, the eternal element in man *and* in all sentient beings, is identical with Ultimate Reality (*brahman*), and hence there can be only one Self. Although this identity has always existed, it has to be realized before a person can be liberated, and thereby released, from implication in the transitory and illusory world and from the notion that one is different to, or separate from, *brahman*.

Sankara gives a number of examples of the illusory nature

of the world, including the well-known one of a piece of rope being mistaken for a snake. In this case, because of the ignorance of the viewer, the illusion of a snake is superimposed on the reality of the rope. Thus our ignorance not only conceals the substratum of the world but also makes it appear to be something else. This concealment and distortion are the two functions of illusion or ignorance (*avidya*).

From the empirical viewpoint *brahman* appears to have many qualities (*saguna*) and to be the creator of the world and its inhabitants; but from the transcendental viewpoint the attributeless *brahman* only is real. This concept of a 'higher truth' distinct from 'ordinary truth' derived from the Madhyamika system of Buddhism. From the empirical point of view *brahman* may be conceived of as a personal creator, Isvara or Visnu, or Saguna-brahman, the transcendental *brahman*, or Absolute without attributes or qualities, is termed *Nirguna-brahman*. Mergence of the individual Self with the *Nirguna-brahman* constitutes liberation.

The devotee begins by worshipping an ideal, a personal deity, (*brahman* personified) which helps to diminish his egotism until finally the collective identity of all beings in *brahman* is experienced. The performance of ritual and the concept of deity is a stepping-stone to the knowledge that God is merely a 'mask' of the impersonal indefinable *brahman*, devoid of all attributes. A long training under the guidance of an enlightened *guru* is the path to liberation; the latter will tell his pupil when he has reached true understanding and will say to him 'Thou art *brahman*'. The pupil will meditate on this until he fully experiences the truth and thereby achieves liberation. Although the liberated Self continues to live in the world he is no longer *of it*, and no appearance, attachment, desire or other emotion can destroy his wisdom and mental equilibrium, since he has given up the illusory notion that he is separate from *brahman*. *Brahman* remains totally unaffected by the plurality of individual phenomena, even as the countless waves of the ocean neither affect nor diminish the ocean's unity.

Some later Vedantins who criticized Sankara's views, including Ramanuja (tenth century) and Madhva, contended that *atman* and *brahman* are relative terms — like part and whole (*visistadvaita*) — and consequently are not identical.

The Visistadvaita school of qualified non-dualism is an important presentation of Vaisnava theology and presents a theistic account of ultimate reality (*brahman*). *Brahman* is the One Reality in which the multiplicity of conscious souls exists, as well as unconscious material objects. Matter exists eternally in *brahman* and from it he spins, like a spider, a web from his own body thereby creating the ephemeral material world. Individual souls are infinitely small, eternal, conscious, and self-luminous, each endowed with a body in accordance with its *karma*. This confinement in a body constitutes bondage; release comes only with the complete separation of the soul from the body. Ignorance causes the soul to identify itself with the body and its desires, sensual pleasures and delights, so it becomes more and more attached to mundane existence and thus continues the long series of rebirths and deaths. The only object worthy of love and devotion is God and constant meditation on Him liberates the devotee. This emphasis on the difference between God and souls was necessary because of Ramanuja's insistence on loving devotion and dependence on Visnu as the 'inner controller' of the individual self. When liberated the soul is *similar* to God but not identical, since that which is finite can never become infinite, yet it shares the same essential nature. None the less nothing exists outside God, for both conscious souls and unconscious matter are within Him. The world, its creatures, and objects are all as real as God, therefore this system is a monism of the One qualified by the presence of many parts.

According to Visistadvaita Vedanta, *brahman* is manifested in five forms: the first and highest is Parabrahman (that is, Narayana-Visnu). Seated on the cosmic serpent Sesa, he dwells in the celestial realm of Vaikuntha accompanied by the goddesses Laksmi, Bhu and Lila who personify prosperity, the earth, and the spontaneous play or self-expression of deity, respectively. This form is enjoyed by liberated souls who become similar to *brahman*. The second form consists of Narayana's three or four emanations (*vyuhas*): Sankarsana, possessor of the qualities of knowledge and the power to maintain; Pradyumna, possessor of the power of ruling and abiding character; and Aniruddha, possessor of creative power (*sakti*) and strength. When a fourth emanation is added, he is named Vasudeva (Krsna) the possessor of all the above six qualities. The third form comprises the ten chief incarnations; the fourth dwells in the heart and accompanies the soul through its series of rebirths to ultimate liberation; the fifth dwells in images during ritual worship.

Some souls gain liberation by undergoing the complex techniques of *karma yoga* and *jnana yoga*, but for the majority such methods are too difficult. Instead they practise complete surrender and loving devotion to God. But Ramanuja did not favour ecstatic devotion; instead he advocated a continuous process of deep meditation on the perfections of God.

By the fourteenth century a number of divisions had occurred among Ramanuja's followers, although all claimed to follow his teachings. These divisions resulted in the establishment of the northern Vadagalai sub-sect, established by the theologian Venkatanatha (also known as Vedanta Desika), which used Sanskrit; and the southern Tengalai, established by Pillai Lokacarya, which favoured the vernacular — so continuing the tradition of the Alvars, the twelve notable poet saints of Tamil Vaisnavism, who lived from the seventh to the tenth centuries AD. The Tengalai stress the importance of divine grace in attaining release; while the Vadagalai hold that submission to the will of God is merely one of a number of possible methods to reach liberation. The Tengalai regard the goddess Laksmi as subordinate to Visnu, whilst the Vadagalai claim that she as well as Visnu are capable of granting liberation.

The chief exponent of the dualist Dvaita Vedanta system was Madhva (1197-1276). According to Dvaita Vedanta God is eternal and both immanent in the world and transcendental to it. The Vedic wind god Vayu is the mediator between God and man and Madhva is regarded as an incarnation of Vayu. The world and souls are also eternal but distinct from one another; and both are entirely dependent on God (Visnu) who rules them and establishes their various states of liberation or damnation according to their *karma*, which represents God's predestinating activity. Liberated souls perpetually adore God but never attain complete union with him; evil souls are damned eternally — a most unusual view for an Indian philosophy, and some Indologists see in it influences from the Christian Syrian Churches.

Some other Vedantic schools are based on minor differences

of interpretation. Most did not have large followings except perhaps that led by the South Indian *vaisnava* Nimbarka who settled at Brindaban and incorporated the Radha-Krsna cult into his teaching. He taught that *brahman*, souls, and the world are identical yet distinct, since even when souls are liberated and merged with *brahman* as energies of God they remain distinct from him. Hence his system is known as Bhedabheda (difference-non-difference) or Dvaitadvaita (dualism-non-dualism) Vedanta, which still has a following in the Mathura region.

Vallabha, also known as Vallabhacharya (fifteenth century) taught an uncompromising doctrine of pure non-dualism, Visuddhadvaita Vedanta. This is very different from Sankara's non-dualism since *maya* is not regarded as illusion but used in its earlier sense as God's creative activity. The world is real and is *brahman* (in this system another name for Krsna). *Brahman* is described as: being, consciousness, and bliss. Individual souls are one with *brahman* and have no separate existence. Vallabha stressed the importance of devotion to God and joy in his creation, and likened the union of Radha and Krsna to the bliss of the soul with God. An important member of this cult was the notable female hymn writer Mira Bai (1498-1573).

The various Vedantic schools have many followers who try to live according to the precepts of the system they favour, and Vedantic teachings still comfort and guide the lives of millions of Indians. Advaita Vedanta is the best known of the Vedantic systems in the West, largely through the efforts of Vivekananda, Radhakrishnan and Aldous Huxley.

Mimamsa

The name of this system means 'critical examination' or 'solution of a problem by reflection'. The early Mimamsa is sometimes called Purvamimamsa, 'earlier exegesis' (of the Vedic scriptures), to distinguish it from the more complex Vedanta called Uttaramimamsa, 'later exegesis', or 'Brahmamimamsa', which concentrates on the teachings of the Upanisads. During the eighth century two sub-schools arose based on the different interpretations of two notable commentators, Kumarila Bhatta and Prabhakara. In many ways Mimamsa views conflict with those of other Vedantic systems.

Mimamsa is an atheistic system attributed to Jaimini and summarized in the *Mimamsasutra* (which dates from the beginning of the first century AD but contains much earlier material). Its main purpose was not with philosophical questions but with the interpretation of the ritualistic aspect of the early Vedic texts, which claim that the sacrificial system is efficacious in itself without the intervention of God or gods. They say that when sacrificial ritual is correctly performed a mysterious potency (*apurva*) arises in the soul which, at an opportune moment, will produce the effect of the action, even though it may be delayed until after the death of the sacrificer. This notion derives from the earlier concept of *brahman* as the power inherent in the sacrifice which keeps the cosmic process going. The Mimamsa also developed a theory of meaning as inherent in sound (*sabda*). Sanskrit, the sacred language of the Vedas, is an emanation of Being (*sat*) in sound, whence comes the inherent power of sacred mantras and of the Vedic hymns.

The Vedas, being divine, must necessarily be free of errors. They are eternal, self-existent and embody eternal laws. Therefore one should perform only good acts advocated in the Vedas, and carry out obligatory rites without desire for reward or merit. Such disinterested action is of prime importance and possible only through knowledge and strict self-discipline, which ultimately destroys the effects of *karma* and leads to liberation after death. If not performed altruistically, the very acts themselves will cause the individual to undergo repeated rebirths before liberation is attained. The initial ideal was the attainment of a state of heavenly bliss, a reward for correct conduct and sacrifice, rather than release from the series of lives, which was a notion that entered Hinduism during the Upanisadic period.

As the Mimamsa system regards the Veda as eternal and unchanging, it was forced to reject the usual cosmological view held almost universally in the Hindu tradition: that worlds periodically come into being, remain for a time and then dissolve into non-manifestation. The world, according to Mimamsa, has always existed and is without beginning or end, since everything in it is formed out of matter which is eternal. There is only an endless process of becoming and passing away and hence no ground for seeing it in terms of evolution and devolution.

The Mimamsa system understands that there are as many souls as there are individual bodies, all formed from matter in accordance with their respective *karmas*. The individual spirit or soul is eternal, because if it perished at the death of the body it would nullify the injunction to perform Vedic rites to attain heaven. However, consciousness is not intrinsic to the soul and only arises in it when associated with a body, and then only when an object is presented to the sense organs. Consequently, when liberated, the soul is disembodied and without consciousness.

8. Yoga

The term yoga means 'to harness' and especially refers to the breaking in of horses and their training and control by harnessing them. It is also applied to various yogic techniques which are intended to 'harness', discipline and perfect one's physical and mental powers — culminating in the intuitive knowledge of the Unity underlying the apparent multiplicity of the world. The term yoga may be applied to all ascetic and meditational techniques, mystical, devotional, erotic or magical. The four main yogic disciplines may be practised whether or not the yogin follows monistic, dualistic, theistic, or pluralistic metaphysics. Ancillary techniques include Hatha, Mantra, Laya, Kundalini and Tantric yogas.

Some forms of yoga are of great antiquity and contain both pre-Aryan aboriginal and Aryan elements. Yogic techniques spread far beyond the sub-continent. Thus the yoga of late Tibetan Buddhism influenced the north Asian and Siberian Shamanisms, especially during the upsurge of Tantrism in the sixth and seventh centuries AD. Yogic concepts also reached Mongolia, China and Japan. Japanese Zen Buddhism is a specific form of yogic meditation. Yogic elements also occur in some forms of Christian mysticism and in Islamic Sufism, although the ideologies of both are diametrically opposed to those of Indian yoga. Yogic aspects were even found among the Celtic tribes although they were stamped out by Christianity. But, in a narrower sense yoga refers primarily to the tenets of the Yoga system of philosophy.

Yoga is referred to indirectly in the Veda in a hymn addressed to 'the long haired one', and in the Upanisads and other works. The *Bhagavadgita* mentions it under its own name. About the time of the *Bhagavadgita* (sixth century BC), a divergence occurred between the teachings of the *Veda* and the *Dharmasastras,* and yogic tenets. The *Dharmasastras* maintain that immortality can be attained only through the performance of one's caste duties coupled with devout worship and the carrying out of religious rites; whereas yoga states that family, home, friends and, in fact, the world must be abandoned to attain not immortality in some heavenly realm, but permanent emergence from the sphere of existence by reabsorption into *brahman.* Such diametrical views naturally caused tensions which the writers of some texts endeavoured to reconcile by maintaining that devotion and ritual worship are suitable for the majority of people, whilst the 'renunciation' required by yoga is for the few capable of achieving liberation by this means. But the tension remains, as can be seen in India today, for although yoga plays an important part in all the spiritual movements of India and yogins are honoured, yet they are never received into the homes of orthodox Hindus.

A *guru* and his initiated pupils are called *sannyasins* 'renouncers', because they have vowed to withdraw from the life of the world. As their numbers are minimal in relation to India's enormous population, Hindu society can provide them with food and shelter, but only outside the village or town since they are ritually impure through not observing the rules of caste. Thus from the moment of his renunciation the *sannyasin* is regarded as one of the walking dead. His wife has the status of a widow and his heirs inherit his property. His only possessions are a straight piece of orange cloth worn as a loin cloth or 'toga', a staff and begging bowl. He must beg only once a day, therefore many of these men suffer from severe malnutrition and related diseases. Some yogins have ritual and sectarian marks made with ashes or coloured earth on the body. The beard, moustache and hair must never be cut.

Some *gurus* spend their lives wandering from place to place, and people attracted by their teachings or holy lifestyle may join them as pupils. Other teachers have groups of pupils and live in *ashrams;* these function on the lines of the European educational system of the Middle Ages, when students paid their professors and lived with them in small communities. In the true *ashram*, caste rules do not apply. Anyone may join and leave whenever he wishes. However, the pupil must provide his own food and shelter. Only initiated disciples are regarded as the *guru's* spiritual sons and therefore perform certain duties for him. There should be no money transactions since everything necessary should come from unsolicited gifts.

Despite the ever growing numbers of Westerners calling themselves 'teachers' of yoga, and the glib way in which yoga is discussed, few study the theory behind yoga — without which it has little value, except perhaps to calm the mind or tone up the body. None of the methods is easy, nor are results achieved quickly, if at all. Furthermore, every minute of one's time should be dedicated to the goal, which even then may elude one since there are countless distractions and obstacles to total reintegration. These include: attachment to the performance of religious rites, or to fame or learning; stealing; lying; causing harm, fear or pain to man or animal; rich living; entertainments; enjoyment of sex; fine clothes; music; literature and amassing money. The main religious obstacles include: becoming immersed in mystical ecstatic states; undertaking pilgrimages; practising extreme mortifications; showing off one's knowledge; desiring to be in the company of holy men; and desiring supranormal physical attainments (*siddhis*) and mistaking their acquisition for full realization.

The mind is easily distracted because it constantly multiplies its activities, thereby dissipating more and more mental energy until the individual loses sight of his goal (*brahman*). Every act has its corresponding mental impregnation, impression or 'latency' (*vasana*), which gives rise to an impregnation of the cosmic value of the forces involved in that action. The impressions begin to accumulate from the beginning of each cycle for each individual and increase proportionately as further mental and physical acts are performed. Thus the individual is 'impregnated' with all the cumulative *karma* of his past lives which will influence his future actions and inclinations in lives to come; but when the yogin draws nearer to his goal the *vasanas* will dissolve.

Desires of every kind constitute obstacles on the path to liberation. Perhaps the greatest is the desire to go on existing. So intense is the will to live that it carries the individual spirit over death to a new incarnation in a new body. Even gods desire to exist eternally, but they too will pass away as do planets, nations, worlds and universes; everything that arises in time must necessarily pass away in time. Paradoxically even the desire for liberation is an obstacle, for the yogin must attain a state of 'desirelessness' before he attains release. In other words he must give up all desire including his desire to attain desirelessness! As the *Yogasutra* states: 'When one enjoys consciousness entirely freed from desire for results, then the true nature of all things becomes clear.'

Withdrawal of the senses from external stimuli stimulates certain 'perfections' or supranormal powers (*siddhis*) which are not created by yoga, for they exist in a latent state in all men, but are brought to fruition only by specific yogic techniques. The 'perfections' include levitation and the capacity to make oneself invisible, or of a small or a vast size. All the 'perfections' appear to be of a purely subjective nature and are not to be regarded as objective realities. The yogin must on no account cling to the 'perfections' but continue on his path of self-perfection and so gain release from the series of rebirths. Even at the beginning of yogic training, the practice of non-injury (*ahimsa*) and kindness to all creatures removes all feelings of fear or hostility when they are in the yogin's presence (*Yogasutra* 2,35f).

With the attainment of liberation the *yogin* is no longer affected by sense stimuli which engender desires, memories and emotions. Henceforth he lives untouched by pleasure, pain, success or failure, disease and other calamities. This complete indifference to the pleasant and the unpleasant resembles the Stoic doctrine of *adiaphoron*, and evidence exists of Eastern influences on the Stoic philosophical school founded about 310 BC by Zeno of Citium.

The first systematic exposition of yoga (known as classical yoga) is attributed to Patanjali, of whom little is known. His *Yogasutras* consist of concise aphorisms giving the metaphysical and doctrinal aspects of yoga, rather than descriptions of the practical exercises intended to assist liberation. He adopted a number of Samkhya metaphysical ideas in his system including the twenty-five principles (*tattvas*) and added another, God or Isvara the 'Lord', as an object of devotion. Isvara (the embodiment of perfection) functions as an example and 'aid' to meditation for those whose temperaments require such an ideal. Ultimately however, the liberated spirit knows nothing of God, who is neither active nor creative having never been implicated in the world process. Sometimes God is identified with, or is interchangeable with, the sacred syllable *OM*.

Patanjali's work was extended by a number of commentators, whose writings have been collated. Philologists who have examined the Sanskrit conclude that he lived just before the beginning of the Christian era, his chief commentator, Vyasa, shortly after. Other important commentators were Vacaspati Mishra (about eighth century), Bhoja (ninth century), Vijnana Bhikshu (sixteenth century), and Ramananda Sarasvati (seventeenth century). None of these teachers refer to the Tantric yogic concepts of *kundalini*, etc.,[1] but all aim at attaining *samadhi*, a withdrawal back into one's inner being. An adept who dies is said to be in *samadhi*. To emphasize the transcendental nature of that state yogins are not cremated after death but buried, there being no way in which it can be ascertained whether or not they are in an extended *samadhi* or are dead. The burial places of notable yogins often become places of pilgrimage.

The many different methods of yoga are not to be regarded as developing stages since the one essential immutable Truth exists forever. The different techniques are but attempts, from different points of view, to comprehend the Unitary nature of Divine Reality.

9. Systems of Yoga

Hatha Yoga

This system is concerned with reintegration through strength; the technique of physical exercise by which the body and vital energies are brought to the highest peak of health and efficiency. This is an essential requirement for the practice of any yogic discipline, for without physical and mental health the goal can never be reached.

Patanjali, in his *Yogasutras*, lists eight stages in Hatha Yoga: abstinences, observances, bodily postures, breath control, withdrawal of the mind from external stimuli, concentration, contemplation and identification or reintegration. These are aided by specific *mudras* and the *bandhas* or muscular contractions (all extremely difficult), and the six internal purifications.

Bodily postures (*asanas*) are important, since mental concentration cannot be achieved unless the body can remain in a comfortable position for at least three hours without fatigue or cramp. The various postures have different effects and can only be learned from a qualified *guru* — never from books. But whichever posture is adopted, the spine, neck and head should be kept erect and the eyes closed or fixed on the tip of the nose, or between the eyebrows. The cross-legged position is not absolutely necessary, but is adopted by Indian yogins because it is the usual sitting position in India. Details of the eighty-four main positions are described in books devoted to yoga. Despite the difficulties of controlling the vital energies, the yogin must remain at all times, gentle, humble and equable, and he must never resort to intoxicants or drugs.

Breath control (*pranayama*) is an important part of yogic technique since breath represents life in its most concrete form, that is, vital energy. Similar techniques are also found in Jainism, Buddhism and Taoism, and were found at one time in the West when the soul was equated with breath. The breath is progressively and rhythmically slowed to bring about very low rates of respiration until the yogin experiences clearly altered states of consciousness normally inaccessible in the waking condition. Complete physiological and psychical control leads to the final state of yogic meditation (*samadhi*) which constitutes liberation. The controlled slowing down of breathing results in diminution of the bodily excretions and other functions but greatly increases perspiration, thus asceticism (*tapas*) is always associated with heat.

Having overcome all physical and mental obstacles, the yogin commences his 'inner' journey towards reintegration which involves deep concentration and meditation. Meditation is of three kinds. The first is material, the fixing of the mind on an image of a deity or on one's guru. Because of the mind's difficulty in reaching the supersensible, it concentrates first on a material form, after which it may proceed to more abstract forms of meditation. The second is luminous meditation, concentrated on the radiance of the Divine or of Nature. The third is subtle meditation, with the mind fixed on the point limit (*bindu*) where the unmanifest becomes manifest. At this stage duality vanishes and meditator and the object meditated upon merge, whereupon the elements of the mind dissolve into the non-dual principle, eternal *brahman*.

Karma Yoga

This is a method of reintegration through right action, good works and right living. It is said to be the easiest discipline and is followed by the majority of Hindus. Every action should be carried out altruistically without attachment to results and in accordance with *dharma*. All external moral and ritual practices are based on right action although, from the transcendental point of view, action itself is neutral and only has a right, wrong, or indifferent effect according to whether or not it leads towards or away from the final goal.

The *Bhagavadgita* describes the meaning of Karma Yoga in the story of Krsna and Arjuna. The latter was a member of the warrior caste (whose duty is to fight), but his courage failed when faced with the necessity of waging war against his relatives and friends. Krsna then explained the necessity of right action carried out without any attachment to its immediate or long term results: 'Thus shalt thou be released from the bonds of actions, fair or foul of fruits; and, liberated . . . thou shalt attain to me [Krsna]' (*Bhagavadgita* 18,56).

Jnana Yoga

This involves reintegration by means of deep study, knowledge and meditation on the sacred texts. The metaphysical knowledge (*jnana*) thus gained is knowledge of ultimate realities enabling the yogin to find, and coincide with, his true centre.

Paradoxically, knowledge is used as a way of getting beyond knowledge to the yogic intuition that awareness and beings are identical, and that any apparent distinction between knower and known is illusory.

Included among the seven stages of Jnana Yoga are: discriminating between the permanent and the transitory; reflecting on the teaching of one's *guru*; meditating regularly; and, lastly, entering the unmanifest stage immersed in the blissful knowledge that all is *brahman*.

Bhakti Yoga

This is a system of reintegration through intense devotion (*bhakti*) to one's chosen deity or to Isvara. Isvara is not a creator, for the world and its inhabitants proceed from the same primordial substance (*prakrti*), but for some people Isvara can function as a model and 'aid' to liberation — for he is essentially the deity of yogins. However, Isvara cannot be summoned by rituals, or devotion, or faith in his 'mercy', since he is devoid of desires and emotions; none the less his essence is instinctively drawn, as it were, to the devotee who seeks emancipation through yoga.

Bhakti Yoga is intended for individuals who have difficulty comprehending the abstract impersonal nature of that which lies beyond mundane experience. It is prominent in the literature of the Vaisnava Pancaratras.

Whatever one loves, that one serves joyfully; and the greater the love, the more complete the devotion until finally both merge. But paradoxically, with the mystical union of the Self with God, the deity is experienced intuitively as oneself. Thus the *Bhagavadgita* (6.29) states that through unswerving devotion to God the yogin 'perceives the common essence in all things . . . the Self in all things and all things in the Self'.

There is a difference between the devotion of the ordinary *bhakti* cults and that of Bhakti Yoga. The former leads the devotee to a heavenly world after many existences, the latter achieves permanent liberation from rebirth.

Mantra Yoga

This is a technique based on the inherent power of sound as revealed by the ancient seers. Its aim is to alter the ordinary state of consciousness, which may be attained by rhythmical repetition (*japa*) of Divine names, and by mantras, each having a different effect.

The supreme mantra and object of meditation is *OM* (*AUM*) which is made up of three elements: the two vowels a and u which, according to Sanskrit phonetics, become o when combined, plus the resonant nasal sound represented by m. *OM* represents existential multiplicity and its underlying unity. It is the sound form of Ultimate Reality (*brahman*) and is all-permeating, 'as the constant reverberation of a bell ringing in the distance . . . he who knows it knows the Veda', (*Dhyanabindu Upanisad*, 1,18). With the constant repetition of *OM*, its meaning may be grasped intuitively and liberation achieved. (*OM* is never used in ordinary conversation.) Another important mantra is the *gayatri* which is said to contain the eternal wisdom of the Vedas. It is repeated by every 'twice-born' (*dvija*) man at his morning and evening devotions. The *gayatri* translated runs: 'We meditate on that excellent light of the divine Sun; may he illuminate our minds.'

According to the *Laws of Manu* (2,85f), mantra *japa* is ten times more effective than any other ritual. It can be performed in a number of ways but success is ensured if a mantra is uttered whilst a devotee circumambulates a sacred tree, garden, temple, or other holy place, whilst keeping the Supreme Being always in mind.

Mantra Yoga has sixteen stages culminating in the realization of the mantra's meaning, whereupon the mind of the yogin dissolves into the deity represented by the mantra, leaving no trace of duality.

Laya Yoga

This involves reintegration by mergence with the Universal Being. It is a method based on the concept that the individual being and the Universal Being are essentially one, therefore all that exists in the universe must also exist in every being. To experience Unity, the cosmic energy Kundalini must be aroused.

Laya Yoga consists of a number of stages culminating in the hearing of the inner sound which obliterates all other sounds. At first innumerable sounds will be heard, until finally come those resembling the tinkling of bells, flutes, lutes, or a bee. The mind should adhere to whichever sound pleased it first and so, by meditating on sound alone, the yogin's mind merges into sound as salt dissolves into water.

Kundalini Yoga

This is a method of reintegration achieved by awakening cosmic energy. Kundalini is synonymous with Sakti, the divine cosmic energy existing in every living being and which keeps the world process going. It has unlimited potential, yet remains unrecognized in most people. A qualified *guru* is necessary to guide an initiated pupil (who must be already proficient in Hatha Yoga), in the way to arouse this inner potentiality. It will then burn away all obstacles to spiritual progress and liberation will be attained. The method used includes the practice of breath-control and reabsorption of semen, techniques also employed in classical yoga and in Tantrism.

Kundalini is likened to a fire or to a female serpent half asleep and curled up with its tail in mouth, and hence Kundalini is called 'she who is curled around upon herself'. When roused she gives rise to the universe after a period of dissolution. Sometimes a serpent is depicted encircling Siva. It symbolizes the dissolution of the world. In most men Kundalini gives off just enough energy to keep them going; but when awakened by an adept she rises through the centres of power (*cakras*) distributed along the spinal column, from the base of the trunk to the apex of the skull, called 'Brahma's crevice' (*Brahmarandhra*), through which the liberated spirit escapes into total isolation. These seven centres of the subtle body are a metaphysical image of the gross body. They 'indicate the confluent points of particular vital forces, the activity of which sets the forces of the gross body in motion, but which remain substantially distinct from them, they subsist after death and contribute to the animation of the fetus at the moment of reincarnation in another body in accordance with the laws of transmigration'.[2] Some letters of the Sanskrit alphabet are visualized on the *cakras* and symbolize creative cosmic energy in the form of the revealed Word (similar to the neo-Platonic 'logos'), or more importantly its sound.

The upward movement of Kundalini arouses intense heat (*tapas*) in the yogin's body. When it reaches the top of the skull the lower limbs become cold.[3] The archaic magical technique of producing 'inner heat' reached its peak in the Shaman's 'mastery of fire', although the 'fire' of Kundalini is on a different plane. By arousing and controlling the forces released, the yogin becomes purified and gains physiological and physical powers leading to liberation.

Tantric Yoga

This is a form of devotional yoga that uses nature to overcome nature, and the body to discipline the body. The yogin endeavours to overcome and so dominate the distractions of the world which stand between him and the Absolute, by using them to destroy the desire for constantly new experiences. Even too great a stress on the performance of religious rites can become an obstacle. For example, Ramakrishna, an ardent worshipper of the goddess Kali, became so immersed and ecstatic in his intense adoration of the goddess that he lost sight of his ultimate aim, which was liberation from every form of attachment. When he understood his error he smashed her image. Later he believed that Kali herself had given him the necessary will-power and strength to carry out this apparently sacrilegious act. Thus by an 'evil' act he overcame the 'evil' of distraction from his goal. Similarly, some of the more extreme erotic Tantric practices are intended to enable the adept to utilize the immense power of sexuality to overcome every vestige of desire in himself; but to be efficacious all such practices *must be carried out in a strictly ritual context.*

In the West, and to a lesser extent in India, such methods are frequently misunderstood as giving rise to unbridled sexual perversions and libertinism, but sensuality and self-seeking remove all hope of liberation. The Tantric aim is likened to a kind of 'eternal orgasm', a state of non-duality without awareness of self versus one's partner — a blissful state where Ultimate Unity is experienced.

Raja Yoga

This, the Royal Way to reintegration, is also called the Yoga of the King of Kings (Rajadhiraja Yoga). The latter refers to one of Siva's titles and indicates Saiva influence on classical Yoga. Siva is the Great Yogin and the presiding deity of yogins. He is also Lord of Sleep and thus represents the final dissolution of individuality and the cessation of self-manifestation.

According to Hindu tradition, Raja Yoga is the supreme yogic form and any genuine yogic method must be subsumed into it. Many ancillary yogas are merely names of the various stages of Royal Yoga, or sub-divisions of a stage as the 'yoga of magic formulas' (Mantra Yoga).

In Raja Yoga the function of the intellect is to control the body and calm the agitation of the mind. After a time the adept sees supramental visions 'and with them comes the perception of the fundamental unity of all that exists; consequently, all things are perceived to be, in their nature, aspects of this unity. If following any river we go down to the ocean in which all rivers unite, we can then go up any river we choose; similarly, if we dive down into ourselves to that point where all beings are one, we can thereafter enter into the most secret heart of all beings or things of the differentiated world.'[4]

Raja Yoga comprises eight (and sometimes fifteen) main stages leading to the acquisition of supranormal powers (*siddhis*), which in themselves may become obstacles on the path to liberation if the yogin allows himself to be carried away by his achievements. Among the stages are: the control of the senses through the knowledge that 'all is *brahman*'; meditation on the basic unity of all things; non-observation of differences; and perception of the transitory nature of the world, culminating in *samadhi* or identification with the Divine, a non-dual state where even the notion of contemplation disappears.

10. The Cult of Visnu

The three main cults of the Hindu Tradition are those of Visnu, Siva and Sakti. These cults are not rivals for their aims are identical, that is, the union of all beings with the one Supreme Being, but their methods of reaching the goal differ.

In a vast country like India, where Hinduism has flourished for over four thousand years, there are bound to be divergences of interpretation and doctrine. Among the multitude of cults and sub-cults (some very small), some flourish, others decline, and others almost disappear; but all claim to derive from the teaching of the Vedas, especially the Upanisads, and to present different views of one and the same truth. This tolerant outlook enables new cults to be assimilated easily with older ones. As Sankaracarya pointed out, the deities worshipped in different religions are but symbols which enable finite minds to grasp the Infinite, or at least some of the aspects of the ineffable reality that is One.

The way of devotion (*bhakti marga*) is the basis of the Vaisnava devotional cults. It gives an entirely different meaning to the Upanisadic concept of the impersonal *brahman* or Absolute. From the devotional point of view, *brahman* is regarded as a personal God or Lord (Isvara), so making a strong appeal to the masses who long for a comforting 'humanized' God ever devoted to their interests.

Single-minded concentration on, and love of, God completely purifies the heart. All thoughts, words and actions of the devotee must be carried out altruistically, regardless of success or failure; one's whole being then becomes rooted in God in whom all desires are fulfilled.

God can be apprehended only intuitively through total devotion to him. As Krsna is made to say in the *Bhagavadgita* (12,8): 'Fix your mind on me alone, concentrate your intellect on me; henceforth you . . . dwell in me alone.' Even so it is only by God's grace that one becomes enlightened and liberated; this is an idea that cuts across the earlier concept of the inexorable law of *karma*, which is an important part of the Hindu tradition. None the less the doctrine of grace is stressed in the *Svetasvatara Upanisad* (6,23), but was not fully developed until the Epics and later devotional works.

Love of God is an end in itself, its visible signs being kindness, gentleness and care for all creation. Both the practice of yoga and true knowledge are necessary to follow the devotional path, for the former concentrates the mind in meditation, while the latter purifies it. The concept of God's grace to humanity was widely disseminated by the theory of God's incarnations (*avataras*) and emanations (*vyuhas*) who appear on earth to aid man and other creatures.

By the seventeenth century the devotional (*bhakti*) movement had reached its peak and was predominantly Vaisnava. But Saivism also produced a devotional cult, which flourished in Bengal, based on the worship of Sakti, Siva's consort and the personification of his cosmic energy. The Sikh religion is also devotional, but it is now separate from the Hindu devotional movements as its members no longer regard themselves as Hindus.

Most of the devotional cults are characterized by rhythmical singing and dancing, when the devotee may experience ecstatic contact with the Divine. The way of devotion is universal and open to all — irrespective of caste, sex or character, since no one can be denied the right to love God. As Ramananda said: 'Let no man ask a man's caste or sect. Whoever adores God is God's own.'

Visnu in the *Rgveda* appears to be an aspect of the sun and is notable for his three great strides from earth, to atmosphere, to the heavens — a cosmic act signifying his might, his pervasiveness and capacity to traverse all regions known and unknown to man. He is the lord of unceasing activity and lord of life. His beneficence extends to man and to all creatures.

The origin of the name Visnu is unknown. The French Indologist Louis Renou[1] suggests that it may be non-Aryan. It is possible that Visnu was originally an important, non-Aryan deity who became incorporated in the Vedic 'pantheon'.

In common with Siva, Visnu is a conflation of many local divinities. These include: an ancient god having some solar characteristics; a popular deified hero, Vasudeva (also called Bhagavat), worshipped in western India (and whose name was said erroneously to be a patronymic of Krsna); and the philosophical Absolute of the Upanisads. This assimilation of deities occurred before the second century BC, since an inscription on a pillar at Besnagar states that the Greek ambassador Heliodorus was a devotee of the 'God of gods' Vasudeva. Vasudeva is said to have propounded the Bhagavata religion which included some solar features and later developed into Vaisnavism. A flute-playing pastoral deity of unknown origin was also identified with the god-hero Krsna who in turn is recognized as an incarnation of Visnu, as are the heroes Parasurama and Rama. The incarnatory theory greatly facilitated the assimilation of popular divinities into Vaisnavism. It developed during the Epic period and is referred to in the Puranas. The latter gave variant lists of incarnations which suggest regional and sectarian preferences.

The stages by which Visnu rose to become a main deity are lost in the distant past, but some clues remain: the *Rgveda* identifies Bhaga, the lord of bounty, with Varuna and later with Visnu; and the *Brahmanas* identify Visnu with the personified Sacrifice and with the Cosmic Man whose sacrificial dismemberment gave rise to the universe. (Sacrifice was the most important of all Vedic rites.)

Both Vaisnavas and Saivas regard their individual supreme deity as a different aspect of the same divine being, since divinity, although essentially unitary, has countless facets. This tolerant attitude is clearly brought out in the *Bhagavadgita* (7,22f): 'If any worshipper do reverence with faith to any god whatever, I make his faith firm, and in that faith he reveres his God and gains his desires, for it is I who bestow them.' Further attempts to harmonize these cults culminated in the triad (*trimurti*) consisting of Brahma (as creator), Visnu (as preserver) and Siva (as destroyer); but essentially the three deities represent different aspects of the unitary Divine. Another syncretism of much greater significance was that of the god Harihara (Hari is a title of Visnu and Hara a title of Siva). Iconographically the two deities are conjoined; the left side of the body represents Visnu, the right, Siva, each with their usual emblems. The Harihara cult has some temples in the Deccan where the god is still worshipped.

Visnu embodies the *guna sattva* (of goodness, truth and light) and the cohesive or centripetal tendency existent in everything which holds the universe together. Visnu is the power by which things exist; whilst Siva represents the centrifugal tendency towards dispersion, decay, annihilation and darkness (*tamas guna*). When Visnu sleeps his cosmic sleep on the shoreless ocean (signifying non-manifestation) he rests on the serpent Sesa ('Remainder') the embodiment of the remnants of the dead universe, until the unfolding of a new one.

Visnu's main symbols are the discus and conch shell. The latter has the form of a multiple spiral arising from one point and opening out into ever-widening spheres. It symbolizes the origin of existence. The discus or six-spoked wheel is a symbol of Universal Mind, 'the limitless power which invents and destroys all the spheres and forms of the universe, the nature of which is to revolve'.[2] Visnu's vehicle (*vahana*) is the enormous human-headed bird Garuda, a survivor of a cult formerly associated with Vasudeva.

Visnu has always been predominantly a gentle, loving god, always near to and mindful of man. His devotees hope to dwell with him after death in his realm Vaikuntha. He is worshipped with flowers, fruit and other simple offerings and no animal sacrifices are allowed. His consort is Laksmi, the personification of beauty and prosperity, and all women are created in her form.

Visnu's Ten Main Incarnations (Avataras)

The incarnatory theory is associated mainly with Visnu in view of his functions of pervasiveness and preservation which presuppose his care of, and interest in, all creation. Siva also has some incarnatory forms of minor importance, which appear to have been introduced in imitation of the Vaisnava incarnations that so greatly appealed to the laity. The Vedic theory that a god, by his creative power (*maya*), can assume any form, human or animal, at will (as did Indra) also influenced the incarnatory doctrine. Visnu is said to 'descend' to earth at different times specifically to re-establish the *dharma* and to punish evildoers when cruelty and corruption are rife. Later a number of partial incarnations occurred, such as Kapila the legendary founder of the Samkhya system.

Theoretically there is no limit to the number of incarnations. The Vaisnava theologians fixed the number of main incarnations at ten but there are some variations in the lists which suggest regional preferences. Images of the incarnations are found throughout India, usually carved on shrines or sometimes depicted on the reverse side of the stone or metal plates (*Visnupattas*) found in eastern India. Some of Visnu's incarnations assume animal form, because in India animals are regarded as reservoirs of power and so may represent the mysterious power of deity.

The ten main incarnations are:

1. **The Fish** (*matsya*) incarnation, whose function was to save mankind from destruction in the Deluge. A miraculous fish warned Manu Satyavrata (the seventh lawgiver and founder of humanity in the present age), of an impending flood, and directed him to build a ship and to embark on it with the sages, animals, plants, and his family. When the storm occurred a huge horned fish would appear to tow the boat to safety. Manu followed the instructions. The fish duly appeared and Manu used the body of the serpent Sesa as a rope and attached it to the horn of the fish who towed the ship to a mountain where it remained until the waters subsided.

It is obvious that both Indian and Hebrew versions of the Deluge are based on the Sumerian Deluge story recorded on a tablet dated about 1750 BC.

2. **The Tortoise** (*kurma*). The tortoise has long played an important part in the cosmogonic and genealogical conceptions of the Indian peoples. It is probable that there were non-Aryan tortoise cults later incorporated into the Hindu tradition.

The upper and lower shell of the tortoise represent the sky and earth respectively, and between the shells, the atmosphere, which signifies Visnu's association with the three divisions of the universe.

The tortoise is said to be the father of all creatures and hence the creator Prajapati assumed tortoise form. As the Lord of Waters the tortoise is identified with Varuna, to whose realm go all creatures who drown. The Tortoise is the mythological basis on which the earth rests; it also served as the support for the churning rod when the gods and genii churned the Ocean of Milk (*samudramathana*), a symbol of the abundance of nature and of all things that benefit man. Because the tortoise can withdraw its limbs into its shell at will, it came to signify those persons who discipline their emotions and senses, remaining always self-controlled and tranquil; it is also a symbol of sacrifice.

3. **The Boar** (*varaha*) incarnation. Visnu assumed this form to rescue the earth, personified as a goddess, from the demonic Hiranyaksa (Golden Eye) who had seized the Earth and placed her in the depths of the ocean. Some texts state that the boar was the mate of the Earth-goddess, a natural notion as the boar in Indo-European mythology is connected with the fertility of the earth and with clouds.

This incarnation may have been influenced by non-Aryan pig or boar cults, such as the popular Boar-god of East Malwa. The *Satapatha Brahmana* gives the boar the non-Aryan name of Emusa. The family emblem of the early Calukya dynasty was a boar, bestowed on them by the grace of Narayana (Visnu).

The Boar incarnation was important in some parts of India in Gupta times. An inscription on a stone image of Varaha found at Eran and dating from about AD 500, records the erection of a temple dedicated to Narayana in boar form.

4. **The Man-Lion** (*Narasimha* or *Nrsimha*). The Man (*nara*) lion (*simha*) incarnation was a cult which flourished during the early centuries AD. Its adherents were mainly kings and warriors because Narasimha embodies courage and bravery.

The pious Vaisnava Prahlada, son of the demonic king of the genii Hiranyakasipu ('Golden Dress'), was persecuted constantly by his father because of his devotion to Visnu. Finally Hiranyakasipu decided to kill his son. Hiranyakasipu himself was invulnerable, Brahma having given him a boon so that he could not be killed by day or night, by god, man or beast; so in order to save Prahlada, Visnu assumed the form of Narasimha. He appeared at twilight from a pillar inside the palace and tore Hiranyakasipu to pieces with his lion claws. (In this context the lion represents brute force.)

Narasimha protects man from the attacks of demons, wild animals, thieves, adverse stellar omens and every kind of peril. The choice of this half-man half-animal incarnation is because man is the most excellent of all creatures, and among the lower animals the lion is the bravest and most powerful.

5. **The Dwarf** (*vamana*). When the virtuous but proud *daitya* king Bali had gained control of the world, the gods became afraid and begged for Visnu's help, whereupon Visnu assumed the form of a dwarf (dwarfs were widely believed to possess miraculous powers), and asked Bali to give him the amount of land that he could cover in three strides. Bali readily agreed to this modest request, but to his amazement the dwarf instantly grew to an immense size and traversed the whole earth in three steps. The last step landed on Bali's head forcing him down to the nether regions. Here, the number three indicates Visnu's universal character, for the universe is tripartite: the upper regions, the earth, and the waters.

To reward his magnanimity and virtue Bali was made ruler of the lower regions. This myth is based on the Vedic story of the solar Visnu's three strides, which in turn probably derives from the Iranian story of the three steps of Amesa-Spenta.

6. **Rama with the axe** (*Parasurama*). Before being adopted into Vaisnavism Rama was an epic hero. According to epigraphic records he was worshipped from the fourth to the eighth centuries. Among his many deeds he re-established the social order when the nobility attempted to wrest spiritual leadership from the priests. If they had been successful human society would be liable to the tyranny of kings, of merchants, or of others. Rama is reputed to have destroyed all the nobles and warriors and established a monarchy controlled by the

priesthood. The story of this incarnation probably refers to the final destruction of the non-Aryan kingdoms.

7. **Rama,** also called *Ramacandra.* This Rama was probably a seventh or eighth century heroic chief associated with the cult of Visnu. He exemplifies courage, virtue, benevolence and duty, and thus is the embodiment of righteousness. Rama's cult includes devotees from all classes of society. His selfless helper and devotee, the monkey demigod Hanuman, is venerated by villagers in northern India, and is also depicted in most of the ancient forts of southern India.

The *Ramayana* describes many of Rama's miraculous adventures and states that he was King of Ayodhya — a realm synonymous with peace, justice and prosperity. Rama's wife is the beautiful Sita, the embodiment of wifely devotion, who was kidnapped by the demonic Ravana, King of Lanka, and later rescued by Rama. Metaphysically she is the mother of the manifested world, whilst Rama signifies non-manifestation. Sita is also regarded as an incarnation of Visnu's wife Laksmi.

This cult became popular soon after the Moslem invasion.

8. **Krsna, the 'Dark One'.** Krsna was an ancient non-Aryan tribal hero of the Yadavas. He was also a teacher who became identified with Narayana (Visnu) and with Vasudeva (originally a separate deity), and consequently was incorporated in the Aryan 'pantheon'. Visnu assumed the form of Krsna to establish the religion of love at the beginning of the present age. A number of legends (some incongruous) from different ages and regions coalesce in the Krsna myth. Krsna is by far the most important of all the incarnatory forms.

Krsna's mother, Devaki, was a sister of the tyrannical King Kamsa. The sage Narada had foretold that the king would be killed by a nephew. Consequently Kamsa kept Devaki captive and killed each one of her six children. The seventh, Balarama escaped, and the eighth, Krsna, was secretly exchanged for the daughter of a cowherd. His idyllic childhood was spent with the pastoralists and he was greatly loved by the cowherd girls (*gopis*). His favourite was Radha (the embodiment of success), daughter of Krsna's foster father Nanda.

A number of mystical erotic cults are based on the love of Krsna and Radha, and during the late Middle Ages devotees often worshipped them together.

The stories of Krsna's many romantic attachments and adventures have been greatly exaggerated over the centuries, largely due to the fertile Indian imagination; but these adventures are intended to show his plenitude of being, which encompasses every part of life, and that he bridges the gulf between God and man. His beauty, kindness and personal magnetism, as well as his overwhelming affection for all living creatures, encourages lesser beings to strive for perfection and liberation. As a child he aroused maternal love in women, as a youth he was the perfect lover. Women's love for Krsna is sometimes interpreted as the soul's desire for God. To men he was the ideal teacher, heroic warrior and ruler.

Krsna's chief queen was Rukmini, daughter of the King of Vidarbha (modern Berar). Krsna founded and ruled wisely the kingdom of Dvaraka in Kathiawar, which was later submerged in a great flood.

The devotional (*bhakti*) cults teach that all human beings may realize their identity with the one reality *brahman* through loving union with Krsna. The *Bhagavata Purana* states: 'To the man who finds delight in me alone, who is self-controlled and even-minded, having no longing in his heart but for me, the whole universe is full of bliss.'[3] Only the truly virtuous can rise above good and evil. Having reached this happy state all actions will be performed altruistically, devoid of any thoughts of merit, demerit or reward. He will desist *naturally* from evil actions and thoughts, and not merely from a sense of sin, or fear of punishment, or fear of accumulating adverse *karma*.

9. **The Buddha.** The Buddha was probably included among the incarnatory forms of Visnu by Vaisnava theologians who were anxious to absorb heterodox cults. Sometimes the Buddha's role is said to be to mislead the unwary and the wicked, but the *Gitagovinda* states that Visnu became the Buddha out of compassion for the sufferings of animals and to prevent bloody sacrifices. This incarnation is seldom worshipped by Vaisnavas.

10. **Kalki or Kalkin.** This is the future incarnation of Visnu, probably based on the earlier Buddhist teaching of the future Buddha Maitreya. Kalki will appear, as a warrior holding a flaming sword and mounted on a white horse, at the end of the present age of cruelty and strife. In southern India he is represented only as a white horse, perhaps a memory of some ancient horse cult of the region and of the power associated with this animal.

The *Mahabharata* describes Kalki as a heroic brahmin who will appear in the future to punish the wicked, and save and comfort the virtuous — a hope especially prevalent among Hindus and Buddhists during the successive Moslem invasions from the eighth century onwards. The desire for a divine deliverer was also common to the ancient world in Egypt, Babylonia and among Jews and Christians.

At the end of the age Kalki will destroy the world to prepare the way for a new and better creation.

Vaisnava Cults

The Bhagavata and Pancaratra cults

Some Indologists claim that initially these two cults were separate, the Pancaratras worshipping the deified sage Narayana, and the Bhagavatas worshipping the deified Vrsni hero Vasudeva: 'the two sects being later amalgamated in an attempt to identify Narayana and Vasudeva; but the names Bhagavata and Vaisnava were sometimes used to indicate Visnu worshippers in general'.[5]

The Bhagavata is a theistic devotional cult which flourished a century or two before the Christian era and which represents the beginning of Vaisnavism. It is based mainly on the *Bhagavata Purana* and *Visnu Purana*, two works very popular during the Gupta period (fourth to the sixth century). The Gupta kings called themselves Bhagavatas and disseminated the cult's teachings in northern India and the Deccan. The adherence of the Rajput kings further spread Bhagavatism to the whole of India. In southern India, in the Tamil land, the Bhagavata movement was spread largely by the twelve Alvars (who had intuitive knowledge of God). They flourished from the eighth to the early years of the ninth century. Their teaching was monotheistic and emotional rather than metaphysical. The Alwars longed for freedom from the series of births and deaths and loving union with Visnu. They sang their devotional songs and hymns as they wandered about the country.

The Alvars belonged to various classes of society. Among them were: a king of Malabar; a famous woman, Andal, to whom a magnificent temple was later built at her birthplace, Srivilliputtur; a low caste man; and a repentant sinner. After the Alvars came the Acaryas, who did not rely solely on devotion, but united it with knowledge and *karma*. They worshipped the Alvars, and in turn were themselves worshipped as incarnations of the Divine. Most of present-day ritual is based on rules laid down by the Alvars.

The supreme deity of the Bhagavatas is Vasudeva (identified with Krsna and Visnu). The devotion inspired by this cult is not as warm or as emotional as that of Caitanya's, being based more on awe and respect than on adoration. According to Megasthenes, in the fourth century BC, Vasudeva was then an object of devotional worship, and therefore the cult must have been established before that date.

The Bhagavata cult was associated with sun worship and its teachings were influenced by the Samkhya-Yoga system. Two important tenets were the need to meditate regularly, and never to injure any living creature.

When the cult reached its peak during the second century AD it came to be generally known as the Pancaratra Agama. The Pancaratra cult is an early ascetic and esoteric devotional movement. The name means 'five nights', but its significance is unknown. A number of suggestions have been made: for example, that it is a name applied either to the Bhagavata cult or to one of its branches since, according to the *Pancaratrasutra*, Narayana performed a five-day sacrifice by which he 'became all beings'; or that it was connected with specific vows formulated five times a year, after the analogy of the seasons.

According to tradition the Pancaratra teachings were first systematized in about AD 100 by Sandilya, who stressed the need for total devotion to Vasudeva-Krsna. Furthermore, a cosmological basis was given to Vasudeva-Krsna by identifying him and the members of his family with specific cosmic emanations (*vyuhas*): this was an important tenet of the early Pancaratras and of the later Sri Vaisnava cult. The emanatory theory developed early in the Christian era, about the same time as the incarnatory theory.

The Pancaratras postulate a supreme personal *brahman* (simultaneously immanent and transcendent), who reveals himself as Visnu, Vasudeva and Narayana and whose power produces the universe. At the beginning of time, the supreme aspect of Vasudeva created from himself the *vyuha* Sankarsana (a name of Krsna's brother) identified with primal matter (*prakrti*). From these two combined, Krsna's son Pradyumna was produced and identified with mind (*manas*). From these arose Aniruddha (Krsna's grandson), identified with self-consciousness (*ahamkara*). From the last two sprang the elements and their qualities (*mahabhutas*), simultaneously with Brahma who fashioned the earth and everything in it from these elements.

These three emanations are regarded not only as aspects of the divine character, but as gods in their own right. Thus paradoxically the gods are both one and many. Later their worship declined when the concept of Visnu's incarnations became popular and dominated Vaisnavism during the Gupta age. All the above deified heroes were worshipped in the Mathura region by people of Yadava-Satvata-Vrsni origin (Krsna was a Yadava), and the teaching was carried to western India and the northern Deccan by migrating Yadava tribes.

Visnu's power (*sakti*) personified is Laksmi, who in essence is identical with him yet distinct as an attribute. She manifests herself as the emanations and projects the world in the second and third stages of creation. This is an attempt to explain the existence of a perfect, pure deity with a limited and transitory creation. In this context Visnu transcends time whilst Laksmi presides over the transient world.

The Vaikhanasa Cult

This was a strongly ritualistic cult which was said to have been founded by the legendary Vikhanas whose teaching was disseminated by four ancient sages: Atri, Marici, Bhrgu and Kasyapa. They composed a number of ritual handbooks advocating devotion to Visnu and worship of his incarnations.

The Vaikhanasa is conservative and stems from the Vedic tradition, many Vedic technical terms being included in the sacred texts as well as Vedic and non-Vedic mantras. Fire oblations are also performed according to Vedic rules. Initially the cult formed part of the Taittiriya school of the *Black Yajurveda*, but later it became an orthodox Vaisnava cult. In its main text, the *Vaikhanasasutra* (dated about the third century AD), the cult of the Vedic solar Visnu coalesces with that of Narayana.

Vaikhanasa ritual theory is based on the fivefold conception of Visnu: as the Supreme Deity; as Purusa, the life principle; as Satya, the static aspect of deity unlimited by time; as Acyuta, the immutable aspect unchanged by any external influence; and as Aniruddha, the irreducible aspect. Performing the fivefold ritual expiates evil and bestows happiness on everyone (and is also a rain spell).

Visnu's ten main incarnatory forms are also worshipped for specific purposes: the Fish and Tortoise to attain indifference to mundane objects and to acquire supranormal yogic power; the Boar for the king's prosperity; the Man-Lion for invincibility and destruction of enemies; the Dwarf and Parasurama to attain a kingdom and also wisdom; Rama for happiness and increase in goodness and virtue; Balarama for sovereignty over the whole world; Krsna for enjoyment, happiness, supremacy and satisfaction; and Kalki for the obstruction of evil.

Image worship is important in this movement and is said to be a development of aniconic Vedic ritual. A large immovable temple image of Visnu represents his transcendent aspect; smaller portable images signify his earthly aspect underlying his various incarnatory forms.

From the end of the tenth century Vaikhanasa priests were in charge of Vaisnava temples, shrines, and lands. Although somewhat eclipsed by the rise of the Sri Vaisnava cult, the priests still perform rituals in the Sanskrit language at some temples, including the Venkatesvara temples at Tirupati and Kanci.

Sri Vaisnava Cult

This cult was founded by Ramanuja, a notable religious and social reformer who was born near Madras in the twelfth century. The cult is an offshoot of the Pancaratra movement which flourished in the Tamil country.

Ramanuja evolved a philosophy of qualified monism (Visistadvaita), a form of Vedanta based on the concept of a loving personal God having attributes and encompassing souls and matter. The human spirit is separate and different from the Supreme Spirit, although dependent on it, because love requires a relationship between lover and loved. Visnu is equated with *brahman* (the Absolute), but in this context *brahman* is not the attributeless *brahman* of the *Upanisads*.

Visnu has two main aspects: as the invincible cause of the world, he is the transcendent supreme spirit; and his visible form is the material creation. Thus he is both creator and creation. As the being of God is inexhaustible, the manifested world is only a part of God for he transcends the world process. Human beings are also a part of God, who so loves his creation that he can even override the effects of the bad *karma* of those persons who truly repent.

Ramanuja wrote long commentaries on the *Brahma Sutras*, the *Bhagavadgita* and the *Upanisads*. He advocated the practice of meditation, kindness, charity, non-injury to all creatures and purification of the body. He admitted that liberation could be attained by knowledge (*jnana yoga*), but stated that it was inferior to that attained by *bhakti yoga* involving total devotion and surrender to Visnu. However, according to Sri Vaisnava beliefs, liberation occurs only after death when the individual soul is freed from the limitations of empirical life.

During Ramanuja's lifetime he himself was worshipped, and no Vaisnava temple is perfect without his image. Another follower was Vedanta Desika (also called Venkatanatha), a brilliant and prolific writer, philosopher and poet, whose reputation was so great that it led to his apotheosis. He was an important member of the Vadagalai school of post-Ramanuja Vaisnavism.

After Ramanuja's death his teaching continued to spread throughout India, strongly influencing later devotional cults. At the end of the fourteenth century two main branches of the Sri Vaisnavas were established: the Vadagalai or northern branch, and the southern Tengalai; they differ mostly over interpretations of doctrine and whether or not Sanskrit or Tamil is the holier language. Today Ramanaja's followers are numerous in the Tamil land, and the cult possesses a literature in both Sanskrit and Tamil.

Nimavat Cult

This was founded by Nimbarka, a southern Indian brahmin who went to Brindaban in northern India. He is sometimes identified with the twelfth-century astronomer Bhaskaracarya.

Nimbarka attempted to establish a link between the Absolute and multiple phenomena. Thus his philosophy is a compromise between dualism and non-dualism and is called dualistic non-dualism (*Dvaita-dvaita* or *Bhedebheda*). In other words it teaches the co-existence of distinction and unity in *brahman*. Every man's spirit is capable of absorption into God's spirit, and God, souls and the world are identical yet distinct. The Supreme Deity is Krsna who may manifest himself directly to some of his devotees; but this will occur only after long meditation on Krsna combined with work, knowledge, devotion, surrender to God and obedience to one's guru.

The notable poet Jayadeva was probably a disciple of Nimbarka. His mystical poem the *Gitagovinda* describes the loves of Krsna and the cowherd girls and it was instrumental in spreading the devotional worship of Krsna.

Madhva Cult

This cult is also called Sad-vaisnava to distinguish it from Ramanuja's Sri Vaisnava cult. It was founded by Madhva, also known as Anandatirtha, who was born near Mangalore in western India in the twelfth century. He expounded a dualist doctrine (*Dvaita Vedanta*) and consequently was much opposed to non-dualist (*advaita*) teachings. Madhva forbade animal sacrifices but allowed sacrifices with substitute rice-meal figures of animals.

The most important of his many writings was a commentary on the *Brahmasutra*, a traditional requirement for the founding of a new Vaisnava cult. He maintained that the whole corpus of the Veda is the absolute truth which reveals Visnu's nature and identifies Visnu with the Upanisadic *brahman*.

Visnu (Hari) is the material as well as the efficient cause of the animate and inanimate world and his agent is the Wind-god Vayu. (Madhva is said to be an incarnation of Vayu who functions as mediator between God and man.) All gods are subordinate to Visnu and subject to decay. The countless human souls or spirits are forever separate from Visnu but relate to him as servant and master, thus he controls them and they may be saved by his grace, especially those who worship him with undivided devotion.

Madhva postulated a doctrine of five-fold eternal distinctions: between souls eternally existent and Visnu who is also eternal; between Visnu and matter; between unchanging self-luminous souls and matter constantly undergoing transformation; between one soul and another; and between one particle of matter and another. All these differences remain even after liberation.

Great attention was paid to dreams since Madhva claimed that, as a result of the divine will, men underwent the effects of past actions during dreams, thus enabling them to remove bad *karma*. Liberation is said to come by immediate, intuitive knowledge of the Divine.

A very unusual and un-Indian feature of Madhva's system is the belief in predestination perhaps due to the influence of the Syrian Christians of Malabar. Madhva states that some people are chosen for liberation, some are eternally damned and others destined to undergo an endless series of rebirths and re-deaths. This cult never had a large following, but it appeals to some of the intellectual classes of southern India.

Vitthala Cult

Also called *Varkari panth*, the 'pilgrim's path', this was a thirteenth-century cult centred on Vitthala (commonly called Vithoba) who was regarded as an incarnation of Krsna. Vitthala appears to have been a famous hero who became identified with Krsna. He is worshipped especially at Pandharpur (formerly a Buddhist stronghold), in the extreme south of Maharashtra where a local cult has grown up at his memorial stone. At Pandharpur he infused part of his essence into a brahmin ascetic named Pundarika or Pundalika, whose filial piety was so intense that it attracted the deity to Pandharpur.

The earliest author associated with this movement was Jnanesvara, composer of many devotional hymns and a commentary on the *Bhagavadgita*. Other followers included the poet Namdev (about 1270-1350) who spent many years in the Punjab where he spread devotional beliefs. Some of his verses are included in the Sikh scriptures. Namdev claimed that asceticism, fasting, pilgrimages and contemplation of the Absolute are futile since God is everywhere, therefore it is necessary only to love and praise him. Another notable follower was Ramdas (1608-81), the teacher and inspirer of Sivaji, who was the leader of Maratha resistance to the Mughals.

At least one annual pilgrimage to Pandharpur was mandatory and more if possible. The places associated with the great poets of the past were visited and their hymns and songs sung, including those of the Maratha national poet Tukaram who did so much to popularize the movement. In time he himself came to be worshipped and a number of miracles are attributed to him.

Vitthala worship is altruistic. God is praised but not asked for special benefits, nor are offerings made, since Vithoba loves all mankind and requires nothing but love in return.

Ramavat or Ramandi Cult

This is a reforming devotional cult founded in northern India by the brahmin Ramananda (born about 1299), who had been a follower of Ramanuja. Ramananda attempted to synthesize the best elements in Hinduism and Islam, including some concepts of the Indian Sufis which appealed to both Hindus and Moslems.

His Supreme Deity is Visnu, in the form of the heroic Rama, who is worshipped either singly or in common with his wife Sita. The monkey-god Hanuman, Rama's great devotee and ally, is also venerated especially for his magical powers. There are no sex or caste distinctions as all worshippers of the true God are equal, but caste rules have to be obeyed outside the cult. The main requirement is that all adherents should be deeply devoted to Rama.

Among Ramananda's twelve chief disciples was the reformer

Kabir, who later founded a separate theistic cult, and two women. Ramananda himself is said to be an incarnation of Rama. All the hymns and religious compositions of this movement are written in one or other of the various Hindi dialects and not in Sanskrit, as the latter is understood only by the learned. Ramananda himself did not write anything, but the two notable poets Surdas and Tulsidas helped to disseminate Ramavat tenets.

Vallabha Cult

This was an important movement founded by the Telegu brahmin Vallabha (1479-1531), during the troubled years of the breakdown of the Delhi Sultanate and the establishment of Mughal rule.

Vallabha was an infant prodigy. As an adult he travelled extensively in India for nine years, engaging in learned disputations with members of other cults. During his lengthy pilgrimages he experienced a vision of Krsna who instructed him to go to Mathura, to an image that had mysteriously appeared on Mount Govardhana. Here Krsna revealed to him the way to liberation through total surrender to the deity. Another time Krsna directed him to marry — a most unusual thing for a spiritual leader — to ensure a line of teachers. He composed a number of works including a commentary on the *Bhagavata Purana*, the last section of which describes Krsna's early life and the teachings of the movement. Vallabha taught a doctrine of pure non-dualism (*Visuddhadvaita*) in which the world is said to be the product of an internal transformation of the Absolute.

This movement is centred on the youthful aspect of Krsna called Bala Krsna, also known as Balgopal the 'boy cowherd', and his amorous exploits with the cowherd girls (*gopis*) of Mathura. This amorous play is interpreted symbolically as intense spiritual devotion for the Divine under the guise of earthly love.

Vallabha regarded the world as real and he identified Krsna with *brahman*. Individual souls, and everything else, are one with *brahman*. This is described as: being, consciousness and bliss (*sat, cit, ananda* respectively) which are not merely qualities but *are brahman*. Therefore, one's body, being a part of the divine, should not be mortified by asceticism but reverenced and enabled to experience pleasure and comfort.

Vallabha postulated three ways to reach liberation: the first two involve continual activity and ritual; the third, the real way, is the 'way of well being' (*pustimarga*) or devotion to Krsna. All selfishness and individuality must be given up and Krsna served devotedly in the home or at his shrines. Krsna dwells in his image during ritual worship and hence the image is dressed and ornamented and flowers offered to it. Music and singing are customary, and on special occasions there is dancing.

Unfortunately many of Vallabha's successors and descendants interpreted his teaching too literally, which gave rise to much immorality and to deviant sexual practices. His successors to the hereditary leadership were called Maharajas, 'Great Kings', who stressed the importance of complete devotion to the guru. In fact, gurus were deified and regarded as incarnations of Krsna which led to further abuses. Every offering was first dedicated to the guru. Even wives and daughters were sometimes offered to them and carnal lovemaking was instituted in many places, ostensibly as a ritual re-enactment of Krsna's mythological erotic exploits. The Maharajas' behaviour continued to degenerate until some reforms were attempted in the nineteenth century, although in India it is almost impossible to alter any social custom having a religious basis. None the less, in 1862 the Maharaja libel trial took place and partly checked some of the cult's more licentious practices.

Caitanya Cult

This was a devotional cult which grew up around the Bengali visionary Caitanya (1486-1533). Initially he was not attracted to the popular devotional movements until he came under the influence of an ascetic who initiated him into the worship of Krsna. He joined a number of devotees who met nightly to sing devotional songs, to have ecstatic visions and to experience possession by the deity. Among other factors that influenced his beliefs were: the *Gitagovinda* of the twelfth-century Sanskrit poet Jayadeva, who described the love, separation and reunion of Krsna with his beloved mistress Radha (Krsna's favourite among the cowherd girls); the erotic songs of the fourteenth-century Maithili poet Vidyapati and those of the Bengali Candidas; and the Tantric Buddhist Sahajiya movement.

The concept of cosmic unity is represented by man and woman in sexual union, the ideal model of divine love and existence being the union of Radha and Krsna in Brindaban. The stories of Krsna's dalliance with the *gopis* became greatly exaggerated over the years. Many of the tales probably derive from stories associated with local tribal deities who became identified with Krsna.

An important feature of Caitanya's movement was the rhythmic and almost hypnotic chanting of songs, sacred names and invocations. A branch of this cult has reached Europe and the United States in the Hare Krishna movement, whose members constantly chant Krsna's names — especially that of Hari, which is said to ensure entry into Krsna's realm.

So intense and absorbing were Caitanya's own devotional ecstasies that he never made any attempt to found a cult himself, but his personal magnetism and intense religious devotion encouraged others to join him during the dark days of the Moslem invasions. His devotees later formed a cult; the six theologians of this cult were called Gosvamins and they codified and expounded Caitanya's beliefs. Caitanya's only known work is a poem of eight verses in Sanskrit, describing his ecstasy in the deity's embrace. Caitanya's highest bliss was to identify himself with Radha that he might experience the passionate embraces of the Lord Krsna.

Caitanya regarded God as the universal male, and the soul in relation to God as female. He is depicted as fair in colouring because Radha was also fair, and Caitanya is said to be an incarnation of her. His followers regard him also as an incarnation of Krsna, or even to be Krsna himself, and consequently he receives intense devotion from them. (Krsna in this movement is worshipped as the Supreme Deity and not merely as an avatar or incarnation of Visnu.)

To identify himself further with Radha, Caitanya frequently dressed as a woman.[5] He taught that the world was not illusory since it is a manifestation of God's power, yet it contains allurements which distract men from realizing their divine heritage.

Caitanya was opposed to caste distinctions as were most

leaders of the devotional cults. Liberation can be attained only by devotion to, and mystical union with, the spirit of Krsna, whereupon the devotee loses all sense of individuality and consequently the problems, limitations and isolation that individuality inevitably brings. Chanting, singing, music and dancing are ways to bring about the desired goal.

Brahman in this movement is not regarded as attributeless (that is as undifferentiated, pure consciousness), but as a personal being possessed of infinite attributes, including all-embracing love and companionship, who is manifested to men in the perfect form of Krsna.

At times Caitanya's intense ecstasies culminated in fainting fits which appear to have affected his reason, and one day he vanished. After his disappearance his followers declared him to be a full incarnation of Krsna, while his two principal followers Advaita and Nityananda were said to be partial incarnations. The triad of Caitanya, Advaita and Nityananda are known as the three Great Lords (Prabhus). Another of Caitanya's companions was Haridas who is worshipped as a separate deity in Bengal.

Caitanya declared that liberation may be attained during life, when the devotee realizes himself as part of God. Although still subject to the effects of previous *karma* it no longer binds him. Total love of God *is* liberation, a state of bliss in which the devotee is united with God.

Kabirpanthi Cult

This is based on the teachings of the poet Kabir who worked as a weaver near Varanasi in the fifteenth century. He was brought up by Moslems and his name is Moslem, but he became a disciple of Ramananda and was instrumental in spreading the Ramandi tenets in northern India.

Kabir attempted to reconcile Hinduism and Islam. He urged his followers to live simple productive lives. Women were admitted into the order after a probationary period. Much of his teaching is a reaction to the excessive ritualism and hair-splitting arguments overlaying both Hinduism and Islam. He rejected most of the outward forms of Hinduism, including the cult of images, caste distinctions, penances, asceticism, fasting and also the six main philosophical systems. However, as a man of limited education it is unlikely that Kabir had much knowledge of Hindu philosophy or of Islamic thought. He stressed that liberation is by devotion alone. He believed in transmigration and that the soul, according to its conduct on earth, enters a heaven or a hell between the successive series of rebirths. The Word was important, both the word of a reliable teacher and of divine inspiration. As Kabir said: 'I am a lover of the Word which has shown me the unseen [God].' He stressed the unity and spiritual nature of the one God whom he called Ram (Rama) and Allah.

Although during his lifetime many Hindus and Moslems disapproved of Kabir, after his death the Hindus wished to cremate his body while the Moslems wanted to bury it. During the quarrelling Kabir is said to have appeared and told the disputants to raise the cloth covering his corpse. This they did to find only a heap of flowers.

After his death the cult divided into two main branches. The Moslem followers of Kabir keep themselves separate from the Hindu adherents. The latter formed the Kabirpanthi sect, which has a large following in north and north-west of India.

A number of collections of Kabir's poems (written in an old form of Hindi) are extant. He describes the difficulties and loneliness of the long spiritual path which leads to ultimate mergence with the One, where all duality vanishes and all opposites are reconciled.

Kabir's teachings and poetry influenced the founder of the Sikh cult Nanak Shah (1469-1538) and some of Kabir's poems are included in the Sikh scripture, the Adi Granth. Kabir also influenced Dadu, the founder of the Dadupanthi movement.

Dadupanthi Cult

This was a reforming movement founded by Dadu (AD 1544-1603), at one time a follower of Kabir. Dadu's writings are known as *Bani*. He rejected caste distinctions, the cult of images, pilgrimages, the authority of the Veda and of the Qur'an, and any other external marks of piety. There is one Supreme God who is creator and teacher whom the devotee must adore and cling to.

Dadu himself lived the life of a householder and did not regard living in the world as an evil, but many of his followers were celibate monks and mendicants.

Svami Narayana Cult

This cult was founded by a brahmin, born about 1780, whose proper name was Sahajananda. He was appalled by the vices and excesses of the leaders of the Vallabha cult, and determined to expose them. Svami Narayana was an upright, generous and ascetic man who attracted many followers, thereby arousing the jealousy of the brahmins of Ahmedabad. This caused him to leave the city for Jetalapur some twelve miles away, where more people joined him. Later he moved to a secluded village and erected a temple to Narayana (that is, Visnu-Krsna) his Supreme Deity. He taught complete devotion to Krsna, observance of one's duties, and pure living. Drinking intoxicants, meat-eating, and killing any creature are forbidden. Pilgrimages to holy places are mandatory, especially to Krsna's city of Dvaraka in Gujarat.

The followers of Svami Narayana are divided into two main groups: Sadhus, celibate 'holy men', and Grhastas 'householders'. In common with many other notable religious leaders Svami Narayana is worshipped by his adherents as a partial incarnation of Visnu.

11. The Cult of Siva

Siva, one of the two great gods of Hinduism is, like Visnu, a composite deity whose origin is lost in the distant past. His ambivalent characteristics derive from the assimilation of a number of originally independent tribal, Dravidian, Aryan and aboriginal deities. His cult includes beliefs ranging from highly spiritual views to quite repulsive practices and rites. Saivism is closely allied to yoga and magic and is given much more to extremes of religious fervour than the cult of Visnu.

Saivism came to the fore in post-Upanisadic times, when it existed amicably side by side with the flourishing Vaisnava cult. Sometimes the two cults overlapped, as in the concept of the triad (*trimurti*) in which Brahma, Visnu and Siva are regarded as the 'three in one', that is, the three manifestations of the One Supreme Being.

As a member of the triad, Siva represents the disintegrating tendency (*tamas guna*) of the world process. Whatever comes into existence, or is born, moves inevitably towards decay and death; this includes the universe which expands for billions of years, only to dissolve ultimately into a state of non-manifestation. But Siva is both the source of the world and its destruction, and he alone remains at the beginning and end of worlds for he is the substratum of existence. Beyond him is only non-existence (*Svetasvatara Upanisad*, 4,18).

Siva is identified with the terrifying Vedic god Rudra. 'Siva' means 'auspicious', a propitiatory euphemism initially applied to Rudra and which later became the proper name of the god Siva.

Saivism has long been the religion of the masses as well as the repository of esoteric doctrines. These have been handed down from generation to generation of initiates, thereby preserving many of the higher forms of metaphysical thought during periods of war, decadence, famine and other calamities.

Siva both creates and embodies all aspects of the dynamism of Nature which carries things forward from birth to death. Hence Siva may be represented as Ardhanarisvara the hermaphrodite (this form also symbolizes the male and female aspects of divine being); or as a bull signifying his virility aspect; or he may be symbolized by the *yoni* and phallus conjoined. Siva as Nature works through man and all other species, but *not for them.* His cosmic functions are performed totally without attachment to their results. Thus he became the model for ascetics and yogins who also strive to perform all actions unmoved by their effects.

Siva brings the fructifying rain and also dangerous floods and crop-destroying hail. The hosts of the dead and howling dogs follow in his wake like the 'Wild Huntsman' of Western mythology. Siva's many names, attributes and epithets indicate his diverse functions. As the personification of the disintegrating power of time, he is called Kala and depicted adorned with garlands of human skulls, his body entwined with snakes symbolizing the cycles of Time. As the passing of time inevitably leads to death he is called Mahakala or Hara the 'Remover'. Consequently he is said to dance in cremation grounds and on battlefields, yet there is hope for his devotees for he is also the death of Death, the bestower of immortality on his devotees. As Lord of Mountains and lonely places he is Girisa. As Lord of Animals and hunters, he is Pasupati who represents the destruction of life by hunting, war and disease; as Lord of Demons (*bhutas*) he is Bhutanatha; as the Supreme Yogin, perfect in austerity and meditation, he is Mahayogi; as guru of yogic knowledge, music and the Veda, he is Daksinamurti, the embodiment of yogic power that destroys the bonds binding the individual spirit to the world and so gives liberation; as the giver of the bliss arising from absolute knowledge he is Sankara; as the transcendent lord of divine knowledge he is Mahesvara. The last signifies the state where all manifestation and differentiation of forms cease. Mahesvara also coordinates the three energies from which knowledge arises, namely: the power of understanding (*jnana*), will (*iccha*), and action (*kriya*). Consequently he is invoked to bestow intellectual achievement on his devotees. As the cosmic Lord of the Dance (Nataraja) he embodies the universal energy expressed in his five activities: the projection or 'creation' of the world; its maintenance; its destruction; the concealment of his nature through the world process; and the granting of grace to his devotees.

The many diverse and sometimes contradictory attributes ascribed to Siva forces the human mind, in its perception of the divine, to go beyond the limited human perspective, and to perceive the inherent inscrutability of the Divine.

Siva is universally worshipped in the form of the phallus (*linga*), the source of manifestation and life, which inevitably contains the seeds of disintegration and death. The female generative organ (*yoni*) represents Siva's Sakti, the personification of his cosmic energy. When represented together the *linga* and the *yoni* signify the two great generative principles of the universe. The same conception may also be represented by his hermaphroditic form Ardhanarisvara, portrayed with the right side of the body male, the left female, denoting the culmination of all male and female forms. Their union in one body signifies the One substratum underlying multiplicity. The early *lingas* were portrayed realistically, but those of the Gupta period onwards are so stylized as to be unrecognizable except by Saivas and others who have studied Saivism.

Some of the Puranas identify the whole of creation with Siva through the doctrine of his five faces — Isana, Tatpurusa, Aghora, Vamadeva and Sadyojata; and his eight forms, originally independent local gods — Sarva, Bhava, Pasupati, Isana, Bhima, Rudra, Mahadeva and Ugra. Siva's five faces are personified as the rulers of the five directions, the four points of the compass and the zenith, making up the totality of spatial extension. The eight forms represent the five elements — ether, air, fire, water, earth — and also sun, moon and the individual self (*jiva*) or sacrificer. From this viewpoint Siva and the world are one. It is a theory rejected by the Saiva Siddhanta cult, whose members regard Siva as Lord of the

World, but different from it in essence since worship demands a subject and an object. The *Svetasvatara Upanisad* states that Siva is both transcendent and immanent, the material and the efficient cause of the universe.

Although Saivism did not develop a complex incarnatory theory, as did Vaisnavism, it none the less regarded Siva as the head of a family of deities each of whom became a cult object. They include Ambika, Siva's wife. She is the Great Mother with whom the 'mothers' (*matrkas*) of later belief are associated, and she is the supreme object of adoration in the Sakta cult. Ambika has many names including Parvati, Uma, Gauri, Durga and Kali. Her figure alone, or with Siva, is depicted on the coins of Huvishka, indicating that she was also a goddess in her own right. Siva's own sons, Skanda and Ganesa, also became cult objects; the latter is still counted among the five major gods and is also worshipped by Vaisnavas. Ganesa, being part-human and part-animal, represents the unity of opposites and the identity of God and man as expressed in the phrase, 'Thou art That' (*tat tvam asi*).

Saivism flourished under the Gupta Dynasty whose rulers came to power in AD 320, although most of them were Vaisnavas. In southern India, the Pallava King Mahendravarman I (who lived about 600-630), was at first a Jaina and later a Saiva. He built a number of magnificent temples dedicated to Siva, an example which was carried on by his successors. Royal patronage greatly increased the popularity of Saivism, as did the mystical and devotional poems composed by the sixty-three Saiva Nayanmars (also called Adiyars). Their poetry is permeated with a sense of the unworthiness of man before the holiness of God, a notion which gave rise to the concept of God's grace to aid the aspirant to gain liberation through total devotion to Siva. By the end of the eleventh century their hymns and poems were collected, and together with other writings, are known as the 'Tamil Veda'.

Saiva ascetics may be recognized by the horizontal painted streaks on their foreheads; Vaisnavas by vertical marks.

In Siva all opposites are reconciled and transcended, good and evil, pleasure and pain, health and disease, life and death. Therefore, Siva may be portrayed as the passionate lover of his consort and at other times as the supreme yogin, wholly removed from all erotic or worldly desires and attachments.

As Nataraja, the king of the dance, he represents the totality of the world process, an omniscient cosmic power ever creating and destroying myriads of creatures.

1. Saiva Cults

The Pasupata

This is probably the earliest known Saiva cult as suggested by the name and Siva's title of Lord of Animals (*pasu* 'animal' and *pati* 'lord'). He aids his creatures to overcome the fetter (*pasa*) of the material world. Originally, Pasupata was a guardian deity of cattle upon which the prosperity and wealth of the community depended. A number of local godlings of herdsmen and agriculturalists were assimilated into Pasupati, which accounts for the cult's popularity in rural communities and with traders. Pasupati is the Herdsman of all creatures, the friend and guide of every species and guardian of the abundance of the earth. The cult flourished in Orissa and in western India from the seventh to the eleventh centuries, and earlier it was established in the island of Java.

The founder or systematizer of the Pasupata cult was Lakulisa, said to be an incarnation of Siva. Lakulisa's special emblem was a club (*lakuta*) which sometimes symbolizes the phallus. He is usually depicted naked and ithyphallic. The latter state does not signify sexual excitement but sexual restraint by means of yogic techniques. The retention of semen is believed to increase a yogin's power and energy.

The cult's main text is the *Pasupatasutra* attributed to Lakulisa. It is primarily concerned with ritual and discipline, and also contains some Samkhya-Yoga and Vaisesika teachings.

According to a thirteenth-century inscription Lakulisa had four chief disciples who founded four subsects. There were a number of Pasupata temples in northern India from about the sixth century, but by the eleventh century the movement was in decline.

The ultimate aim of the cult is to attain eternal union with Siva and thereby overcome all pain and suffering. Among the stages to this goal are: to serve in a temple and wear only one garment, or to be naked. The body is marked with sacred ashes, here representing the *semen virile* of Siva. Siva, whose body is 'made of energy', is worshipped and imitated. The devotee dances frantically, laughs, and roars like a bull, which is said to enable him to attain yogic powers, including a Shamanic type of possession by the deity. Later he leaves the temple, removes the sectarian marks, and behaves in an idiotic or indecent way, thereby inviting the ridicule and disgust of orthodox Hindus. The ridicule of others counteracts the devotee's own bad karmic effects and transfers to him the merit of those who scorn him. The indecent behaviour was a means of cutting off the devotee from ordinary society and producing in him a state of tranquil detachment, and hence he should live in a cave, derelict building or cremation ground. The remaining stages consist of increasingly difficult ascetic practices leading to total control of the senses. A number of striking resemblances between the religious practices of the Pasupatas and the Cynics have been pointed out by Ingalls.[1]

After a long hard training the aspirant attains a superhuman body like Siva's and shares his omnipotence and nature — a view that indicates Tantric and Shamanic elements in the cult. But Siva is eternally and wholly independent of matter and of souls which are dependent on, and eternally associated with, him. The Pasupata movement is the only one to link liberation with the attainment of supranormal powers.

Saiva Siddhanta ('Saiva doctrine')

Also called Agamanta Saiva cult, this is an important southern Indian system of pluralistic realism. It recognizes the reality of the world and the plurality of souls. Siva is its Supreme Deity, who exists eternally and is unaffected by the dissolution or arising of worlds.

This movement developed partly from the 'songs' of the early Saiva 'saints' to whom Siva's grace had been mystically revealed, and partly from the fine devotional poetry of the Nayanmars (from the seventh to the tenth century), the counterparts of the Vaisnava Alvars.

The four classes of authoritative texts of the cult are: the Vedas; the twenty-eight Saiva Agamas; the twelve Timurai; and the fourteen Saiva Siddhanta Sastras. Although the Vedas are highly regarded, the esoteric Agamas are of greater importance having been revealed by Siva himself to his devotees. The Siddhanta Sastras were written during the thirteenth to the early part of the fourteenth century by a succession of six teachers, most of whom were non-brahmins and of lowly origin. They were opposed to caste distinctions which was one reason for the cult's popularity. Another factor was that most of its literature was in Tamil instead of Sanskrit. The Tamil texts and poems include those written by the three great Saiva teachers: Appar, Tirujnana-Sambandhar and Sundaramurti.

The first systematizer of the teaching of Tamil Saivism was Meykantar, in the thirteenth century, in his work the *Sivajnanabodham.* Reality is comprised of Pati, the Lord and personal creator, *pasu* soul (literally 'animal'), and *pasa* 'bond', that is matter. The soul is bound to matter from which it can be rescued only by Siva's grace (*prasada*), a view that cuts across the doctrine of *karma.* To be worthy to receive grace the devotee must perform particular ascetic practices, deep meditation, and be totally devoted to Siva as saviour. With the bestowal of grace the soul mystically realizes its true nature in Siva.

The cult's cosmology is complex and based partly on the twenty-four *tattvas* of the Samkhya system, and on the five *sivatattvas* (pure principles) and seven *vidyatattvas* (categories of knowledge). The *sivatattvas* are *not* identical with Siva who, being transcendent, must necessarily be immutable; but they are acted upon by his energy (*sakti*) and so transformed into the material world and its inhabitants. Although the Lord illuminates souls and supports matter, he is not affected by either. The adherents of this system claim that it is superior to that of the Samkhya, for the extra *tattvas* give them the knowledge of more truths.

The soul is eternal, formless and all-pervading. Its pervasiveness enables it to become one with its temporal dwelling place. Therefore, if it assimilates to itself materialistic things, it will have predominantly gross characteristics, thereby removing it further and further from God; whereas when assimilated to God it will have divine characteristics. Although the soul can know nothing of itself, knowledge of the Divine can be gained only by Siva's grace. Therefore the devotee becomes either intelligent or unintelligent according to whether or not Siva enables him to realize his grace which, although immanent in every soul, yet remains dormant in many because obscured by egotism. Siva takes possession of the completely 'spiritualized' soul which becomes *like* him, sharing his bliss and wisdom, but retaining individual consciousness. This dualistic view is common to all the devotional cults where union with God never means the annihilation of the individual soul, as in the Vedantic non-dual doctrine of total mergence with *brahman*. The Saiva Siddhanta goal is a state of eternal bliss, the experience of unity-in-duality.

Today Saiva Siddhanta flourishes mostly in Tamil-speaking areas including northern Ceylon.

Kashmir Saivism

This is a monistic system, also called the Trika ('threefold') system, expounded in Kashmir by Abhinava Gupta (AD 993-1015) who based his exposition on the teachings of earlier sages. He composed a number of commentaries on the now lost *Sivadrsti* of Somananda, from whom he was fourth in succession. Fortunately a summary of this work was composed by Utpala, a pupil of Abhinava, entitled the *Pratyabhijna Sutras*.

Another teacher, Vasugupta (who lived in the ninth century), taught that the soul gains knowledge by means of intense yogic meditation. This gives rise to a vision of Parama-Siva (the 'highest Siva'), the supreme soul of the universe, whereupon the individual soul is absorbed mystically in Siva.

The name Trika refers to the three-fold scripture drawn from the non-canonical *Agamas*. The system was influenced by Samkhya, Advaita Vedanta and Pancaratra doctrines. There are also some similarities with the teachings of southern Indian Saivism, although from the philosophical standpoint there are many differences; the Kashmir school being idealistic, the other pluralistic in its metaphysical beliefs. Possibly Kashmiri Saivas took the teaching to southern India.

Initiation in this system is of foremost importance. By means of Siva's divine grace the aspirant finds a true guru who initiates him. Thus the 'power of activity' (*kriyasakti*) is awakened in his soul, and this leads ultimately to liberation.

Siva is the *atman* in all beings and objects as well as the universe as a whole. From his pure essence, which is eternal unitary consciousness, the universe and everything in it is projected. Therefore every being and thing is an aspect of ultimate reality. The individual soul or spirit is the limitation of the Divine through ignorance. Siva's consciousness, although essentially unlimited and free, can choose to limit itself by projecting other entities and later absorbing them. 'By the power of *maya* objects which owe their existence to consciousness appear independent of it, thus losing its characteristic omniscience, just as the limitation involved removed the omnipotence. The manifestation of the universe is thus an appearance, not totally unreal as in Advaita Vedanta, but only an aspect of . . . ultimate reality.'[2] Siva being eternal and immutable remains unaffected, his real nature obscured by his *maya;* but when the devotee realizes his identity with Siva, release is ensured. Siva's transcendent aspect is unknowable, but his immanent aspect is manifested as his Sakti (although they are basically one).

Sivadvaita

A system expounded by Srikantha, it has some features similar to those of Saiva Siddhanta and Kashmir Saivism, as well as some unique characteristics.

Srikantha's teaching is based on the *Vedantasara.* The Supreme Siva (Para-Siva) is identified with *brahman* — the material and the operative cause of the world. The latter is manifested through *brahman's* power Para Sakti, the embodiment of wisdom, strength and cosmic energy. Liberation is attained by deep meditation on Siva and this leads to the knowledge that Siva is identical with the individual self. In this way one goes beyond all limitations by identifying oneself with the Unlimited. Regular daily meditation is all-important, for one becomes that which one meditates on.

At death the liberated soul travels along the path of the gods, and passes over the river Viraja beyond which lies Siva's realm. On reaching the river all impurities fall away and final liberation is attained. The soul now enjoys a bliss far greater than anything experienced on earth, for at last its real nature is manifested and it becomes self-luminous.

Kapalika and Kalamukha Cults

These are two extreme Tantric cults, opposed to the teaching of the Vedas, which flourished from about the tenth to the thirteenth century mainly in Mysore. They were probably offshoots of the Pasupata movement. They reduced the diversity of creation into two elements: the Lord and creator, and the creation that emanated from him.

Unfortunately none of their works are extant, but from the seventh century onwards sensational and disparaging allusions are made to them in the Puranas and other literature.

According to a few inscriptions and literary references the Kapalika originated in about the sixth century in the Deccan or in southern India. By the eighth century they began to spread northwards; but by the fourteenth century they had almost died out, their decline being hastened by the rise of the popular Lingayat movement, or perhaps they merged with other Saivite Tantric orders such as the Kanphatas and the Aghoris.

The Kapalikas ('Skull bearers') were adherents of an ancient ascetic order centred on the worship of the terrific aspects of Siva: namely, Mahakala (Time as the destroyer) and Kapalabhrt ('he who carries a skull'), and Bhairava. They were much preoccupied with magical practices, and attaining the 'perfections' (*siddhis*). All social and religious conventions were deliberately flouted, which naturally upset orthodox Hindus: they ate meat, drank intoxicants, and practised ritual sexual union as a means of achieving consubstantiality with Siva and experiencing his divine bliss when in union with Sakti. Many of the sexual rites took place during spring and autumn and probably stem from archaic, pre-Indo-European vegetal cults. The devotees ate from bowls fashioned from human skulls and worshiped Siva, to whom offerings are made in a wine jar. They may carry a triple staff, pot, and a small staff with a skull-shaped top (khatvanja).

Most orthodox Hindus, including Madhva and Ramanuja, rejected these 'fringe' movements because their followers lived licentious lives contrary to the divinely appointed social order or *dharma*. But the excesses and cruelties of the so-called 'left' Tantric cults are based on the notion that man cannot be completely free until the limitations of the laws and ethics of conventional society are transcended.

The teachings of both cults are similar. Both took the Great Vow (*mahavrata*) whose significance is now unknown, and yoga was mandatory. Human sacrifices and wine were offered to

Bhairava and his consort Candika.

The Kalamukhas flourished in the Karnataka area from about the eleventh to the thirteenth century. They drank from cups fashioned from human skulls as a reminder of man's ephemeral nature, and smeared their bodies with the ashes of cremated corpses.

Aghori Cult

This was an aberrant Tantric movement, now extinct, said to have consisted of two branches: the pure (*suddhs*) and the dirty (*malins*). The Aghoris were the successors of the Kapalika cult. Among the female divinities worshipped were Sitala, Parnagiri Devi (the tutelary goddess of ascetics), and Kali. Gurus were highly venerated as is usual in Tantrism.

No religious or caste distinctions were allowed, nor was image-worship, and all adherents were required to be celibate. Cannibalism, animal sacrifices and other cruel rites were practised. All kinds of refuse was eaten including excrement (but never horse meat). As excrement is seen to fertilize the soil, so eating it was thought to 'fertilize' the mind and render it capable of every kind of meditation.

The Aghoris led the wandering life of vagabonds. Each guru was accompanied by a dog, as was Siva in his terrific aspect of Bhairava. The Aghori yogins were buried and not cremated, and were believed to be in a state of eternal, deep meditation.

Virasaiva ('Heroic Saivism')

A southern Indian devotional cult, also called the Lingayat Cult, this was a form of qualified non-dualism, Visistadvaita, which became prominent in the twelfth century. Although the Virasaiva main scriptural text, the *Sunyasampadane*, does not mention the name Lingayat it is probable that originally it was an epithet applied to Virasaivas by other cults, because of their concentration on the *lingam* as the only true symbol of divinity.

Basava was the founder, or more probably the systematizer, of the movement. He was born into a devout Saiva brahmin family, but from an early age he rejected many of the orthodox practices, including investiture with the sacred thread. At sixteen he left home and went to the pilgrimage town of Samgama, where he worked to reform Saivism and to overcome caste distinctions, the ban on the remarriage of widows, and sacrifices. Later he became a minister of the usurper King Vijjala who reigned at Kalyani. Whilst serving the king he converted a number of Jains to his cult. But his unorthodox views caused tension between the king and his subjects and he left the king's service. After Basava's death in 1168 the members of his sect were persecuted but today the movement has many followers, mostly in Andhra Pradesh and Mysore.

A model of the *lingam* is presented to each devotee at initiation and worshipped daily. It is worn in a container round the neck or held in the hand during worship. The Virasaiva initiation replaces the investiture with the sacred thread and this initiation usually takes place during infancy. When a child is received into the community the initiating guru looks intently into the child's eyes and places his hand on his head. 'Through this act he is believed to extract the spiritual principle from the child's body and to place it in the *linga* which has already been consecrated by him . . . This important rite is considered to be a spiritual rebirth.'[3]

Although all wearers of the *lingam* are equal in the eyes of God, some caste distinctions did creep in later. Basava taught that all men are temples, and hence they may worship Siva directly without the aid of priests, ritual sacrifices, fasts or pilgrimages. But again this cult later inaugurated their own priests called *jangamas*, who are regarded as incarnations of Siva. The movement has no temples except those erected as memorials. The rules and ceremonies are similar to those of brahmanic ritual. Women have equality with men and may choose their husbands.

In this cult it is believed that the world and souls are projected from out of Siva's own substance. The soul's main function is to return to its origin. This is achieved by initiation by a guru, continual meditation on, and worship of, Siva, especially in the form of the *lingam* which signifies the origin of life and death and the beginning and ending of worlds without number.

Among the things forbidden to cult members are: pride, dishonesty, meanness, animal sacrifices, eating meat and drinking intoxicants, astrology, child marriage, sexual licence, and cremation. The last is forbidden because at death the devotee goes immediately to Siva and at all times is ensured of his protection. (The dead are buried in a sitting position facing north, unmarried people in a reclining position.) The members of this cult are known for their high morals and ethical behaviour.

Kanphata Yogis or Gorakhnathis

Gorakhnath, a native of eastern Bengal, reorganized the earlier teachings of this movement. He is identified with Siva by his followers. Gorakhnath was probably a notable historical person who lived about the ninth century AD, and who was accredited with great magical and alchemical powers. He synthesized the Pasupata teachings with those of Tantrism and Yoga.

This extreme order of ascetics is characterized by their split ears (*kan* 'ear', *phata* 'split'), and huge earrings of agate, horn or glass, conferred on them at their initiation.

The origin of the order is obscure. Its adherents trace their tenets to a period much earlier than that of Gorakhnath with whom the Hatha Yoga techniques are traditionally linked. The yogis themselves refer to their discipline as Hatha Yoga, although the term later designated the methods used to gain total mastery of the body. The yogis practised ritual copulation in graveyards and sometimes cannibalism. They are said to dwell in jungles surrounded by tigers which serve as their mounts. The tiger in Shamanism is the 'master of initiation' in Central Asia, Indonesia, and in other areas where it is believed to carry the initiate into the jungle, a symbol of the beyond.[4] This order also includes elements from Saivism, the Upanisads, Tantric Buddhism, Vedanta and magical and aboriginal beliefs; consequently it appealed particularly to the slightly 'Hinduized' masses. The ultimate aim of the devotee is to attain eternal union with Siva by means of yogic techniques. Some texts mention thirty-two yogic positions (*asanas*); the *Siva Samhita* lists eighty-four, all having magical and hygienic value. Some destroy sickness, old age and death, while others confer spiritual perfections (*siddhis*).

The Nine Nathas and the eighty-four Siddhas play an important part in the movement and much folklore is associated with them. Their interpretation of the ancient teachings 'finally complete the synthesis among the elements of [Mahayana Buddhist] Vajrayana, and Sivaist tantrism, magic, alchemy and Hatha Yoga'.[5]

Gorakhnath's teaching is universal and hence opposed to caste distinctions. There are few prohibitions concerning food, except that beef and pork are forbidden. But, spirits and opium may be consumed and yogis are allowed to marry. The dead are buried in the posture of meditation for they are permanently in *samadhi*, and hence their tombs are called *samadh*. Representations of the *linga* and *yoni* are placed above the tomb. The *linga* hallows the tomb and signifies that the deceased has identified himself with Siva, therefore the tomb no longer contains a corpse but a 'liberated one' in an eternal state of deep meditation.

Kanphata yogis officiate in temples dedicated to Bhairava (a horrific form of Siva), Sakti or Devi, and Siva. At one time the Gorakhnathis were associated with the Aghoris, who practised a number of revolting rites.

Today the Gorakhnathis are in decline both in India and in Nepal where, in the latter part of the eighteenth century, they received royal patronage, Gorakhnath being the clan god of the Gorkha dynasty who unified Nepal.

12. The Sakta Cult

Although Saktism and Tantrism were originally two different cultural forces, they are now closely associated. Both are centred on the worship of the Supreme Goddess Sakti (representing creative power) as the feminization of Ultimate Reality (*brahman*). In her manifested form Sakti personifies the power of divine Being, the activating principle of existence. Thus to members of these cults God is conceived as female; a concept which, until recently, was almost incomprehensible to Westerners reared in the Semitic patriarchal tradition. However, a Roman Catholic theologian has stated that God cannot be defined as male, female, or neuter, but as all three.[1] This is in line with Indian thinking because the Divine ultimately represents the Absolute and hence can never be qualified in any way, being beyond all polarities. Consequently, in the Hindu tradition it is permissible to worship God in male, female, or neuter form, or as formless, according to the spiritual level and natural inclination of the individual worshipper.

The roots of the Sakta cults go back to a prehistoric Earth cultus, the Earth being conceived as a religious form which developed into the notion of the Earth as the Great Mother, the repository and source of all manifestations, potentialities and powers. The popular Indian village tutelary goddesses (*gramadevatas*) are extensions of the concept of the great Mother Goddess.

A number of other archaic elements have been assimilated

to the Great Goddess, some from India's complex tribal cults and others from the Dravidian and Indus Valley Civilizations. The fact that Sakti (the generic name of the Goddess Devi) is known by so many names shows her composite nature, which incorporates the functions of many local and tribal goddesses.

Although Saktism is closely associated with Saivism, it is none the less distinguishable from it. This is despite the fact that the concept of Sakti, as the Supreme Power of the universe, appears fully developed in the Saiva *Svetasvatara Upanisad.*

As early as the *Rgveda* (10.125) the goddess Vac represents cosmic energy, later deified as Sakti. Similarly, Indra's consort Saci also personifies divine power. The *Atharvaveda* makes a brief reference to Gnas (literally 'women'), which suggests that the powers of nature were associated with female energies long before the advent of Tantric teachings. The Gnas were probably divinities belonging to the vegetal and fertility cults of non-Aryan India. Gonda[2] suggests that from an early date the term Sakti conveyed the idea of an energy by which man might ritually come into contact with the Divine.

The concept of universal energy and the mysterious power of woman, as a productive and destructive force, played an important part in the idea of the Great Mother Goddess, the source of the phenomenal world. She embodies the vast energy manifested in the overflowing abundance of Nature and the totality of the world process, both physical and psychical. Thus Sakti is active and immanent in the world process whilst Siva is inactive and transcendent. When this concept is represented iconographically Siva, identified with the Cosmic Man Purusa, lies motionless 'like a corpse' under the feet of the dynamic Sakti Kali, identified with Nature (*prakrti*) who represents the projected energy of God. Without the polarity and ultimate union of these two principles nothing in the world can occur. In this context Siva represents eternity and Sakti time, and their union signifies the mystery of creation from the Unmanifest (*brahman*). Another symbolic representation of Siva and Sakti is that of the *linga* (= Siva), and the female generative organ (*yoni* = Sakti) combined, signifying the basic unity underlying the apparent multiplicity of the universe. This unity is also represented by the Ardhanarisvara hermaphrodite form combining Siva and Parvati (Sakti) in one figure.

By the seventh century, in Bengal, a number of local goddess cults, including those of Manasa, Sitala and Candi (goddess of hunters), had been assimilated to the worship of Kali, who later became identified with Parvati, Siva's consort.

Among Sakti's many names is Durga-Kali. Her cult in Bengal is a mixture of deep devotion, holiness and religious awe coupled with revoltingly cruel blood rites deriving from an ancient tribal cultus. She is also the tree deity Vana Durga, associated with the ghost tree (*pisacadruma*) especially worshipped by women. Her vegetal aspect can be seen also in the autumnal ceremony of Navapatrika (the Nine Plants) in each of which dwells one of Durga's nine forms who protect her worshippers. When signifying abstract Time, Durga-Kali is called Adyasakti — the primordial active female principle in which no duality exists and all opposites are reconciled. This indicates her unmanifested state before the unfolding of a new world, but as soon as the creative process starts, distinctions arise in the manifested form of the Goddess. At the dissolution of the world (*pralaya*) at the end of the age, Sakti again becomes Adyasakti the Unmanifested non-dual principle, neither male, female, neuter, nor hermaphrodite.

As Time (*kala*) does not exist until the Goddess manifests herself, she is called the 'mother of Time' (Kalamata); as the embodiment of the total creation she is Mahakali; as destroyer of worlds and of Time she is Kalaharsini. But whatever name or form she assumes her quintessence remains unchanged.

The lunar aspect of Kali-Durga symbolizes astro-cosmic totality, and hence she may be depicted iconographically with sixteen arms, signifying the sixteen digits of the moon, which correspond to the Vedic belief that the universe is made up of sixteen parts. In another aspect she is associated with blood, life, and the sap of plants from which arise new life forms in an unceasing generative process. The sacrifice of goats and buffaloes is said to be especially pleasing to her. The unfortunate animals are secured to a sacred pillar, a symbol of the division between life, death and creation, from chaos, that is, non-manifestation before forms are differentiated.

At one time animal sacrifice was common in most Hindu temples, but it gradually declined with the advent of

Buddhism and Jainism and their emphasis on non-injury (*ahimsa*). Today it is found only in some remote tribal cults and in a few temples dedicated to Kali or Durga, or to the terrible forms of Siva. The majority of Hindus, as well as most Saktas, highly disapprove of it. Now the idea is, as the Baul song says:

to light the lamp of knowledge, offer the incense of an earnest soul; then only will that one who is divine fulfil all your desires/ Wild buffaloes and goats, these are the Mother's children; she does not want them as sacrifice/ If you would offer Sacrifice, then stay your selfishness, and lay your love of ease upon the altar/ . . . Where men make caste distinct from caste there can be no Sakti worship. Let all the castes be one and call to her as Mother, else will the Mother never grant us mercy.

When Sakti is portrayed with Siva as his consort her aspect is beneficent and she is called Parvati, Devi, or Uma the embodiment of ideal womanhood, or Mahadevi the Great Goddess. The eternal blissful union (*samarasya*) of Siva and Sakti is the basis of the 'realistic monism' of the Sakta and Saiva cults.

13. Tantrism

This is a form of sacramental ritualism, having a number of esoteric and magical aspects, which employs mantras, *yantras* and yogic techniques. Tantric elements also feature in Jainism, Mahayana Buddhism, Saivism, Vaisnavism and Saktism. Many Tantric beliefs, which vary regionally, spread to Tibet, Turkestan, China, etc. Eliade points out that 'more than one curious parallel can be noted between Tantrism and the great Western mysteriosophic current that, at the beginning of the Christian era, arose from the confluence of Gnosticism, Hermeticism, Greco-Egyptian alchemy, and the traditions of the Mysteries.'[1]

The name Tantrism is derived from the sacred texts called Tantras. The earliest works of this vast literature were written during the Gupta Period, although much earlier material is included. To Tantrists, the Tantras are as authoritative as the Vedas and hence are known as the 'fifth Veda'. Tantrism developed primarily in north-west India along the Afghan border and in western Bengal and Assam, all only slightly 'Hinduized' areas of the sub-continent, and hence many non-Aryan features were included.

Initiation (*diksa*) and the receiving of a specific mantra from a qualified guru is all-important in the Tantric cults. The initiate is 'reborn' and given the necessary esoteric knowledge to guide him towards liberation. New forms of asceticism were developed, including the sublimation of sexual union in imitation of the union of Siva and Sakti; this signifies the reintegration of the primordial polarity from which rose the world of multiplicity.

Great power is said to result from the worship of Sakti, but from the philosophical point of view the emergence of the Goddess is the result of the low level of spirituality in the present degenerate age. Hence only 'sexuality' can be utilized to attain transcendence.

Tantrism has two main divisions: the so-called 'left-hand' (*vamacara*) cult and the 'right-hand' (*daksinacara*) cult. The practices of the latter are not as extreme as those of the Vamacaris, and their rites, although similar to the Vamacara, are never performed physically but only symbolically. Neither cult recognizes caste distinctions and all aspirants have to undergo complex initiatory rites. The Vamacara adepts deliberately flout all the social rules and prohibitions of Hinduism *under ritual conditions,* in an attempt to free themselves from the limitations of mundane existence and so attain greater spiritual power. Such excesses are only a minute part of Tantrism although they have received disproportionate attention from Westerners.

Initially the erotic and esoteric aspects of Tantrism were intended only for the fully initiated to use as liberating techniques, although they derive from early orgiastic fertility rites. The ancient belief in the efficacy of sexual rites to promote fertility was common to many cultures. In parts of Europe during the nineteenth century it was customary for agriculturalists to dance naked, or to copulate in the fields, to produce the energy needed to fructify the earth. In Tantric ritual copulation, the female partner (who incorporates Sakti) should be worshipped with deep devotion, and the sexual rites performed without losing one's purity, keeping one's mind uninvolved. Otherwise it would remain on the level of distraction and attachment which prevents liberation.

In the highest form of Tantric meditation the female generative organ (*yoni*) symbolizes the Universal Womb, the source of all existence. When liberated, the souls merge with the cosmic essence in the joy of pure consciousness — being no longer limited by earthly existence.

According to Tantric teaching the only person fit to worship a deity is another deity, therefore initiates undergo many purifications, yogic techniques and the repetition of mantras (sounds having sacramental and magical efficacy). *Yantras*, geometric symbolic patterns having great spiritual significance, are also employed. They are equivalent to the concrete personal expression of the unapproachable Divine. *Yantras* operate in the visible sphere as mantras do in the audible. By means of *yantras* devotees are able to participate ritually in the powers of the universe, and to attain their aims. The best known is the *sriyantra* consisting of a number of interlocking triangles with a central point (*bindu*) symbolizing the eternal, undifferentiated principle (*brahman*), or the world axis seen from above.

The Sahajiya Tantrists reject the use of mantras, texts, images, and meditation, since only *sunya* (the void) is one's true nature. The difficulty in defining *sunya*, and its metaphysical ambiguity, encouraged many extreme sexual excesses; but despite this, the true Tantric way is never easy and requires a long training. None the less, most Hindus disapprove strongly of the erotic side of the Tantric cults.

14. Images, Symbols and Mounts of the Gods

A vast and complex symbolism is associated with Indian images, of which only a small fragment can be explained in this short outline of Hinduism.[1]

Indian images and religious paintings are basically 'pictures' of various aspects of religious belief, which function as aids to meditation and the understanding of spiritual truths. Therefore an image is designed primarily to express ideas rather than to portray the likeness of anything. It should be regarded as a reflected image of the Supreme Being, although from the philosophical viewpoint the godhead is necessarily formless and devoid of attributes. But few people are able to worship an abstraction and therefore the inconceivable Reality is conceived of as a Being with attributes, the creator, preserver and destroyer of the cosmos. During worship the image is said to be suffused with the presence of God, and it is God who is worshipped, not the image itself.

Most educated Hindus are aware that images are symbols and do not regard them as actual living entities endowed with magical powers. Thus the large, beautifully-made clay figures of gods are thrown into rivers or left to decay after worship. However, the more spiritually advanced *yogis* have no need of images, being adepts in techniques which enable them to experience directly abstract entities by inner visualizations and thus to perceive God in their own hearts.

Early Buddhism and Jainism were opposed to the use of

images, preferring to venerate great teachers and sages as visible forms through which transcendent reality may be comprehended. A few Hindu religious leaders including Kabir were also against the worship of images, but the majority of Hindus find them of great assistance in their spiritual quest.

Gods are conceived of in gentle and in terrifying forms to reflect the dualism of the terrestrial world. They are envisaged also under a number of different names and forms. Thus Siva as the Supreme Deity is called Mahadeva; as the Cosmic Dancer, Nataraja; as Cosmic Time present before existence, Mahakala; as the Supreme Yogin and teacher, Daksinamurti; and as the androgyne, Ardhanarisvara.

Siva's main symbol is the *linga* denoting cosmic energy, transcendental power and pure consciousness. His main emblem is the trident (*trisula*) signifying the three *gunas* or 'instruments' of the evolutionary process.

The Indian artist-craftsmen never indulged their individual views and eccentricities, being bound by iconographical rules laid down by priests, although variations do occur especially during the early periods of image-making. After the tenth century fewer variations occur and once one knows the vehicles or mounts of the gods, their emblems, *mudras,* and attributes, it is easy to identify the deity depicted. The gods are usually portrayed with the physical anatomy, such as musculature, not much emphasized, but with broad, well-developed chests denoting the inwardly held breath, the essence of life, controlled by yogic techniques. Their facial expressions are usually inward looking, calm and detached giving a feeling of timelessness. Their figures are somewhat soft and effeminate, signifying the male and female characteristics present in every individual. Each part of an image has some symbolic significance, even to the type of sculptural relief used, and includes the position of the body, the ornaments, attributes, garments and plinth, as well as any accompanying animals, birds, fish, plants and emblems. For as the universe is divinely created, everything in it is necessarily worthy of worship. Some deities are portrayed with more than one head and many arms; this is a device employed to distinguish them from human beings, to indicate their transcendental mode of being and the immense incomprehensible potentiality of the Divine.

The creator Brahma is portrayed with four heads, each

facing a different direction to indicate he is all-seeing and all-knowing. His mount or vehicle (*vahana*) is the snow white goose (*hamsa*) symbolizing the 'One Spirit' or cosmic life force pervading the earth, waters, atmosphere and heavens, for the goose is at home in all these regions. Its whiteness denotes purity, and its graceful, lofty flight is likened to the spiritual efforts of the devout Hindu to attain *brahman*. It is also the bird mask of the creative principle embodied in Brahma. The latter holds the 'Wisdom Vase' a symbol of the earth, the sustainer of all things. Brahma represents the perfect balance of Nature that prevents the excessive predominance of one thing over another. From the initial equilibrium, that is non-manifestation, all opposing tendencies, species and forces develop evenly.

Visnu embodies the *sattvaguna* of truth, goodness and mercy. On his breast shines the brilliant *kaustubha* gem that symbolizes the consciousness of all beings, which manifests itself in all that shines. A tuft of golden hair called *srivatsa* (beloved of fortune) is portrayed on his left breast and this denotes basic Nature, the source of the world. His *makara*-shaped earrings denote intellectual knowledge and intuitive perception; his crown, the Unknowable Reality; and the three strands of his sacred thread represent the three letters forming the sacred mantra *AUM*. His dark complexion denotes the infinite formless, pervasive substance of the spatial universe.

Visnu's special emblems are the wheel or discus, conch, lotus (or bow), and a club. The wheel is a symbol of the boundless power of Visnu's mind and the cohesive tendency holding all composite things together; the conch represents the five elements denoting the origin of existence and eternal space; the lotus the causal power of illusion from which the universe arises and the purity of eternal *dharma*, the basis on which existence unfolds; the club signifies primeval knowledge and the power that ensures conformity to universal law.

Vehicles or Mounts of the Gods

Most gods have animal mounts which are seldom shared with other divinities. Hence these are a more reliable iconographic guide to the identity of a particular deity than are attributes and emblems. Goddesses usually have the same mounts as their consorts.

The animal mount originally may have been the theriomorphic form of the deity. Zimmer[2] maintains that a mount 'is a duplicate representation of the energy and character of the god'.

Siva's mount is the white bull Nandi — the embodiment of moral and religious duty, law and justice, all qualities of the strong. He is depicted white, for that is what remains when all colours have disappeared. Visnu's mount is the mythical bird Garuda, the personification of the sun and wind, of courage, and the esoteric teaching of the Vedas; Agni's mount is a goat or ram, denoting his generative power; and Durga's is a lion, signifying her invincibility and power over enemies. The *makara* symbolizing the life force of the waters is the vehicle of Varuna and Ganga; the peacock, symbol of immortality and love, is the mount of Karttikeya, lord of immortality and of Kama; the rat or mouse, representing tenacity of purpose and the overcoming of obstacles, is Ganesa's vehicle; and the tortoise, symbol of stability, is the vehicle of the Earth Goddess and of Yamuna.

15. Temples

During Vedic times there were no temples or images. Most rites were conducted in the open air or in temporary structures, and were of a sacrificial nature, until post-Upanisadic times when temples were erected. Their design was influenced by the Buddhist Caitya halls and rock-cut sanctuaries dating from the third century BC, a style which continued to dominate architectural forms for over a thousand years. Some smaller shrines are connected with the ever popular Naga cults.

Today no free-standing pre-Gupta Hindu temples remain, for they were built of perishable materials and have long since disappeared.

An Indian temple is primarily the dwelling place of the deity to whom the temple is dedicated. Temples vary in size and shape from a crude shelter made of leafy branches over an image or symbol of a deity, or a simple square cell based on a plinth and surmounted by a spire, to vast temple complexes covering many acres. Priests and their assistants are attached to each temple, but there are no fixed hours and days for worship for the laity: for a Hindu can worship anywhere, at any time, at home, in villages, towns, or in the country. Attendance at a temple is an individual act. Most worship is non-congregational, although collective singing of hymns is popular, especially in Bengal, and was much favoured by Caitanya and by members of other devotional cults.

The main temple-building period took place during the seventh century onwards. The two main styles are: the Dravidian of southern India, and the northern or Indo-Aryan. Most of the finest northern Indian temples were destroyed by Moslems from the eleventh century onwards, but fortunately they failed to reach Orissa and southern India until much later when their iconoclastic zeal had somewhat lessened. The chief Orissan monuments are situated in and around the towns of Bhubanesa and Puri, one of the finest being the Lingaraja temple, another the temple of Visnu Jagannatha, and another the 'Black Pagoda' of Konarak (built in the thirteenth century).

Northern temples are characterized by pyramidal, curvilinear towers with rounded tops, erected on a polygonal base in the centre of which the inner sanctum is placed in direct alignment with the top of the main tower, if there are more than one. The undecorated inner sanctum or *garbhagrha* (literally 'womb house') contains the image of the deity to which the temple is dedicated. This small cave-like cell has no light except that entering from the doorway. Only priests are allowed to enter this 'holy of holies'. Worshippers may approach it along an east-west axis, and in bigger temples through a number of rooms, whose sanctity increases the closer one comes to the inner sanctum, as the worshipper moves from the visual multiplicity of the world to the One Reality. It is customary for devotees to circumambulate the sanctum in a clockwise direction, along a passage built for the purpose. Circumambulation is an act of reverence and gains merit for the worshipper. From the centre of the sanctum the immense power and energy of the deity radiates outwards to the four directions with which specific deities are associated. The guardian deities (*dikpalas*) of the eight directions of space are positioned round some temples. They also play an important part in the design of cities and temples, since much Indian architecture is based on the square, a symbol of the Absolute, fixed by the cardinal points. In addition small altars may be placed under trees, outside temples or at crossroads.

Although temples and image worship superseded the earlier Vedic sacrificial religion, much Vedic symbolism survives. The delineation of the temple area (especially in southern Indian Dravidian temples) reflects the Vedic sacrificial area. The cell and plinth symbolize the Vedic fire altar and the fuel from which the fire leaps heavenwards, or it may signify Mount Meru the centre of the universe. In larger temple complexes there may be shrines, subordinate to the main temple, which are dedicated to other deities. Some 'empty' sanctuaries are also provided where the devotee may invoke his own chosen divinity (*istadevata*).

Southern Indian temples usually resemble a rectangular truncated pyramid, the area being bounded by high walls and big gateways (*gopuram*) surmounted by huge, elaborately carved pyramidal superstructures, often higher than those in the centre of the temple complex. Most of the larger Indian temples give a feeling of stability and strength and appear to grow up naturally from the earth, like great mountains. Architecturally both Vaisnava and Saiva temples are the same and can be distinguished only by the image in the main shrine.

Very complex rituals are connected with the choice of the site for a temple, which may be situated in a grove or other secluded area, and near water (or with a water tank), so essential for ritual ablutions. The ground plan is an architechtonic *mandala* representing the essential structure of the universe. Sometimes the *mandala* is divided into squares with the 'creator' Brahma occupying the central square, and other planetary and astronomical deities occupying the remaining squares. Alternatively, the *mandala* may contain the form of the Cosmic Man (Vastupurusa), the personification of the ideal design of a temple or house. Vastupurusa's figure is arranged diagonally across the squares, each square being connected with some portion of his body. In Indian thought the basis of the universe is considered to be mathematical; thus it is essential that every part of a temple must be correctly proportioned to harmonize with the universe and so ensure its continued state of perfection. Indeed, there are strict canons of architecture laid down in the *Silpa Sastras.* Various building materials are associated with different classes: stone and wood for gods, kings, brahmins and ascetics; brick and wood for the temples of goddesses. If the above three materials are combined the temple is neuter. Re-use of temple materials is prohibited (although it often occurs), because the materials function effectively only in their original context.

A few large temples have been erected in recent times, including one at Delhi and one at Benaras Hindu University.

In principle temples are open to all, except for the inner sanctum, but some are run by societies with private funds and to all and intents and purposes are private property.

A Basic Temple Plan

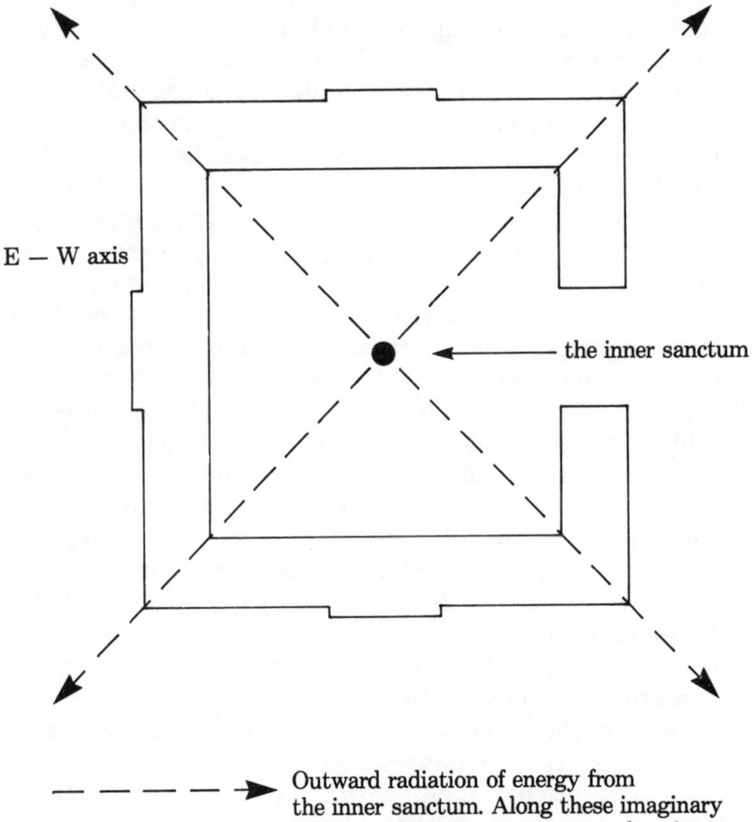

Outward radiation of energy from the inner sanctum. Along these imaginary lines are placed important secondary images of the deity enshrined in the centre sanctum.

16. The Priesthood

The major class of priests are called *brahmanas*. They are members of the sacerdotal and learned caste who possess hereditary rights to perform religious and secular ceremonies, and to expound the Veda and subsidiary disciplines. So complex were the Vedic sacrificial rituals that only priests understood them, which considerably enhanced their status and power.

The Sanskrit term *brahmana* initially meant 'one possessed of *brahman*', the mysterious magical force that pervades and transcends the world. At one time the priests became so powerful that they were regarded as gods in human form and their anger was more to be feared than a venomous serpent. According to the *Laws of Manu* (formulated in about the first century AD) 'the very birth of a brahmin is the eternal incarnation of the Law'.

Although the temple cults of classical Hinduism differ from the Vedic system of worship, the priests came to dominate many of the popular kinds of worship. Even at village level brahmins perform various rites as well as practising as astrologers, healers, etc. However, without the priests with their learning and prodigious memories the oral transmission of the Vedas and other texts would never have survived.

When the brahmins became too numerous for them all to become priests, some entered trade or a profession. This change from sacerdotal to secular work was one of the factors that lessened their power and mystique. Other factors included: the rise of Tantrism with its initiatory rites performed by *gurus*; the tribal groups, on the fringe of the Hindu tradition, with non-Hindu sacraments; the Virasaivas with their own priests called *jangamas*; and finally the rise of the medieval devotional cults which opposed caste distinctions and advocated religious egalitarianism, so enabling popular non-brahmin teachers to obtain followers.

Today, priests perform the rituals of birth, initiation, marriage, and death, especially for the upper classes. Brahmins also perform rites for non-Hindus including Jainas and others.

17. Worship (Puja)

Vedic worship was bound up primarily with the regular performance of sacrifices on which the world process was thought to depend. In classical Hinduism devotional religion came to the fore as the Vedic worship lost ground. Many temples were built and the use of images became widespread, together with the increase in ceremonies, festivals and pilgrimage centres; but some Vedic ritual remains in use among the upper classes, mostly for domestic or social ceremonies such as marriage.

Before an image is worshipped it has to be endowed with breath (*pranapratistha*) that is, life. When this rite has been performed the image is, during ritual, 'god himself', being filled with the vital breath of the deity it represents.

Occasionally worshippers may request boons, but usually worship is more an act of homage, prayer and reverence; the deity is treated like an honoured guest and offered flowers, fruit, cakes or rice. Repetition of the god's name and the uttering of mantras are the main part of many rites and prayer; the more complex forms of worship are performed by officiants (*pujaris*) who attend the deity and carry out the required ritual.

Festivals

Hindu festivals and holy days are innumerable, especially as many Hindus customarily attend festivals associated with deities other than their own chosen divinity, since to the Indian mind all gods are but different aspects of the One Divine.

Most festivals are seasonal and of great antiquity. An example is the Indramahotsava, 'the raising of Indra's standard', the standard being a decorated tree trunk (without branches) set up in the town seven days before the full moon of the month *asvina* (September to October). For the duration of the ceremony the trunk is regarded as Indra himself, then on the seventh day it is taken down, dismantled and thrown into a river. A very popular spring festival is the Holi, which is dedicated to Krsna, Kama and the *gopis,* when the customary rules of behaviour are disregarded. It probably superseded an earlier kind of Saturnalia, as it includes erotic games, folk-dancing, singing of suggestive songs, jumping over bonfires and throwing coloured water over everyone in sight. Sometimes the Holi merges with the Swing Festival (Dola) at Puri (Orissa), during which images of the deity are swung, to increase the fertility of the land.

The chief Tamil festival is Pongal (January to February), when several deities are offered rice boiled in milk, and cows decorated with garlands are led in processions. The main autumn festival is the Diwali or Dipavali (festival of lights) when Laksmi and Krsna are honoured. Lights are set up everywhere and tiny paper boats bearing lights are floated down the rivers.

Every twelfth year the great Kumbha Mela festival is held at Prayaga (Allahabad), when hundreds of thousands of pilgrims gather to bathe at the confluence of the Jumna and Ganges; similar ceremonies are also held at Hardwar, Nasik and other places.

In Bengal the Durga *puja* in October to November precedes the first-fruits festival at which rice is cooked and cattle garlanded. During the festival large numbers of animals, chiefly goats, are slaughtered in the Kalighat temple (Calcutta), and their heads piled up in front of the image of Durga. She is an aboriginal goddess whose worship combines a number of savage tribal elements and practices, including animal sacrifice which is strongly disapproved of by most Hindus.

Other local and regional festivals include the Jagganath at Puri which venerates Visnu as master of the world. His image is pulled through the streets, from the temple, on a huge chariot for several days to commemorate Visnu/Krsna's journey from

Gokula to Mathura. Other ceremonies take place at Kanci, and at Madurai where Siva's local spouse Minaksi, the 'Fish-eyed' goddess (originally a separate divinity), is honoured. Every lunar month the festival of Siva (Sivaratri) is celebrated. The birthdays of notable teachers and sages are also commemorated, including those of Sankara, Ramanuja and Ramananda.

Pilgrimages

For centuries pilgrimages have been, and still are, very popular, for they are undertaken to gain religious merit or to expiate sins. Some involve long and arduous journeys of hundreds of miles, often on foot. The movement of so many people, *yogis* and holy men is a major factor in the dissemination of religious ideas. There are innumerable places of pilgrimage, but the main centres are: Benaras, Hardwar, Ujjain, Mathura, Ayodhya, Puri, Dwarka and Conjeeveram. Benaras, in particular, has 1,500 temples where every cult is represented.

The pilgrims purify themselves by bathing at sacred places, such as the confluence of two rivers, or in the Ganges, the holiest of rivers, from its source in the Himalayas to its mouth in the Bay of Bengal. Some stretches of the Ganges are holier than others, such as Gangotri where the river leaves the mountains, Hardwar where the Gangadvara temple is situated, and Prayaga at the confluence of the Ganges and Jumna.

It is customary to circumambulate various shrines, temples or other sacred objects as an act of respect and reverence. Temples are reverenced in this way because they represent the visible body of the invisible deity. Circumambulation may involve traversing the whole circuit of a sacred area including the *panchkosi*, a fifty-mile-long holy road with hundreds of shrines, which encircles Benaras.

An especially holy centre for Vaisnavas is Brindaban, the birthplace of Krsna. Consequently every part of it, as well as the surrounding area, is sacred including the dust — for on this ground Krsna once trod.

Other cult areas called *tirthas* are usually situated on river banks. They may be a shrine, large tree, mound, or any place associated with gods, goddesses or sages. The place-names of the *tirthas* are often those of aboriginal godlings and cults which were long since absorbed into the major cults.

18. Modern Reformers

The two greatest traumas experienced by the inhabitants of the subcontinent were the series of invasions by the Moslems, and the advent of Europeans in 1498. At first the Portuguese, and later the Dutch and English trading companies, were interested primarily in capturing the immensely rich mercantile trade between Europe and the East, rather than making territorial gains. Consequently, their presence made little impact on Indian society. But this state of affairs changed drastically during the middle of the eighteenth century when the Europeans, especially the French and English, fought each other and also fought the rulers of the Indian states that had arisen on the ruins of the Mughal Empire after Aurangzib's death in 1707. Finally the British conquered their European rivals, but the powerful Marathas remained unconquered until 1818.

During the nineteenth century British influence mainly affected the educated urban middle classes who were exposed to Western political and social concepts, although in their own homes they retained their traditional values and religious practices. However, a number of cults arose at this time as a reaction to the upheavals caused by the European intrusion. Some Indians uncritically accepted anything Western, whilst others vehemently rejected all Western values and ideas. Still others, including Rammodan Roy, Keshab Chandra Sen, the Tagores, Vivekananda, Aurobindo Ghose, Ranade and Gandhi, recognizing the weaknesses of some aspects of Hinduism, tried to counter them by employing both Western and Indian ideals. The intellectual ferment caused by the meeting, or rather collision, of European and Indian cultures stimulated Hinduism to reassert and revitalize itself.

Although the Hindu tradition has assimilated many tribal and other divinities, the gods of the 'Untouchables' were never accepted into the Hindu 'pantheon'. To members of the four main castes, as well as to those of the vast number of sub-castes, the caste system was a divine institution and therefore perfect and unalterable. Consequently to all caste members the 'Untouchables' were a source of pollution. Any contact with them necessitated purificatory rites. Hence many of these unfortunates at the bottom of the social pyramid had nothing to lose by joining one or other of the reform movements, all of which were opposed to caste distinctions.

The first reform movement was the Brahmo Samaj founded in 1828 by the learned patriot Ramohan Roy (1772-1833), who was a revenue official in the employ of the East India Company until his retirement in 1815 when he concentrated on religious and social reforms. He stressed always that he was not founding a new sect but purifying the old religion of its undesirable accretions. Most of his wealth was devoted to the Brahmo Samaj, to philanthropic work, and to encouraging unity between the members of all religions by blending the best elements of Eastern and Western cultures. He believed implicitly in the inevitability of progress based on the scientific revolution, and in Christianity, which appeared to have brought tremendous power and success to Europeans.

Roy's own family were followers of Caitanya. His childhood was spent in Patna, an Islamic centre of learning which doubtless influenced his detestation of idolatry. He was also influenced by Sufism, and the theism of the Upanisads and Vedanta, but he rejected transmigration. Parts of Christianity were adopted, including the Sermon on the Mount, the ethical teaching of the New Testament and the unity of the godhead; but he could not accept the doctrine that Christ was the son of God. During the years 1820-23 he often engaged in controversies with Christian missionaries, in an attempt to correct their totally erroneous views concerning Hinduism.

Roy also devoted himself to removing the many disabilities

suffered by women, including the burning of widows (made illegal in 1829), and child-marriage. Furthermore he modernized the archaic Indian system of education, and in 1816 established the Vedanta College in Calcutta, 'for the propagation and defence of Hindu Unitarianism'.

Roy's successor was Debendranath Tagore (1817-1905) who revitalized the Brahmo Samaj, as well as founding the Truth Teaching Society (Tattva bodhini Sabha), whose members met regularly for prayer and religious discussions. Tagore (in common with other reformers), selected material from the Upanisads, Mahabharata and elsewhere, if it was in agreement with his views.

Keshab Chandra Sen (1838-1884) joined the Brahmo Samaj in 1857. Tagore was greatly attracted to the young man, later to become the third and most dynamic leader of the movement. Sen emphasized the devotional side of Hinduism as well as accepting the divinity of the 'Asian Christ'. He regarded the Old Testament as the First Dispensation, the New Testament as the second, and his movement as the Third. But after his death the movement disintegrated, although the secessionists continued to carry out social work.

Many of Sen's social reforms greatly upset his more conservative followers and caused a split in the movement. Sen and his supporters then founded their own society called the 'General' Brahmo Samaj, whilst Tagore changed the name of his party to Adi Samaj (the 'original' Brahmo Samaj).

After visiting England in 1870 Sen set about the education and emancipation of women, although he allowed his daughter to marry a Hindu prince according to orthodox rites. He claimed to have received a 'revelation' that he should do so. Nevertheless this caused a further schism.

The Radha Soami Movement has Hindu and Sikh affinities and claims to be a universal movement that may be followed by the adherents of any religion. It originated in the teachings of the banker and vaisnava Shiv Dayal (1818-78) which stressed the union between Radha (symbolizing the soul) and Soami (Swami) and the Master, that is God. He also taught a form of yoga based on the creative word emanating from the Supreme Being.

After Shiv Dayal's death the movement split into two, one centre continuing at Agra, the other on the banks of the Beas river near Amritsar. The latter group was supported by a number of Hindus and Sikhs although there are many divergences from orthodox Sikhism.

The Prarthana Samaj of Bombay was led by the lawyer Mahadev Govind Ranade (1842-1901). He continued the monotheistic devotional movement of the Maratha 'saints' coupled with a great deal of social work.

The learned Saiva Svami Dayananda Sarasvati (1824-1883) established the Arya Samaj at Bombay in 1875 and at Lahore in 1877, his aim being to restore Indian culture to its original dignity. His *guru* had impressed upon him the necessity of studying and understanding the wisdom of the Veda which had long been misinterpreted. He therefore based his teaching primarily on the *Rgveda* and to a lesser extent on the Sama and Yajur Vedas, but did not include the *Brahmanas* or *Upanisads.* He pointed out that the Vedas make no mention of the caste system, child-marriage, the seclusion of widows, image-worship, pilgrimages, or incantations. None the less, he did accept the doctrines of *karma* and rebirth although both concepts are post-Vedic. He advocated the worship of the one formless God, service to one's elders and to the community. Women were accorded the high status they had enjoyed in Vedic times as the helpmates of men in religious, public and private life. 'Untouchability' was non-Vedic and consequently thousands of 'Untouchables' joined the movement and were invested with the sacred thread. This enabled them to enjoy the same social rights as caste Hindus but only in the Arya Samaj; outside it they must revert to their usual low status. Non-Hindus are also admitted to the Society. Unfortunately, many of its members have been murdered for their beliefs by fanatics. The movement flourished, particularly in the Punjab where later it played an important part in the Nationalist struggle.

After the Svami's death the society split into two groups: one wanted modern education and freedom of diet, and aimed to establish the Arya Samaj as the nucleus of a world religion; whilst the other group remained conservative. The latter insisted on the infallibility of the Veda, *karma*, rebirth, and the sacredness of the cow. Anti-Christian and anti-Moslem propaganda was promulgated by both groups and in 1947, when India was partitioned, the Moslems took their revenge by killing every member of the Lahore headquarters that could be found, as well as confiscating all the society's property.

A predominantly political leader was Bal Gangadhar Tilak (1856-1920) who advocated regaining political supremacy by non-cooperation with the British.

A further stimulus to Hinduism was given by the Bengali brahmin and mystic, Ramakrishna (1834-1886). His aim was to live a pure, devotional and simple life based on Hindu tenets, and causing no harm to any creature; he was a man of highly spiritual and sensitive character. Ramakrishna's intense devotionalism, and desire to experience every aspect of the Divine, led him to recognize the goddess Kali and other Hindu divinities, as well as the Buddha, Christ and Allah. Throughout his lifetime he saw visions of Kali, Radha and Sita (Rama's devoted wife), whereupon he would experience the joys of married bliss. After studying the New Testament he received a vision of Christ and, when in the company of Moslems, he saw Muhammad. Although he accepted Christ as a son of God or as an incarnation of Visnu, he rejected the claim that Christ was unique as he considered this view to be divisive and hence evil. As a result of his wide variety of religious experiences he assumed that basically all deities are identical and hence there is no need for synthesis, each individual being free to follow the path of his choice to Oneness (*brahman*).

Ramakrishna married when he was a *sannyasin* vowed to perpetual chastity, so the marriage was never consummated. He declared that sexuality militated against spirituality, as did the desire for wealth and possessions. He regarded all women as the 'Holy Mother', Kali.

Ramakrishna taught his followers to realize and develop the divine potentiality within them. When this is attained, the conventional concepts of good and evil cease to have meaning, for the devotee knows that what is good is good because it is God. God is all things.

Ramakrishna's chief disciples were Keshab Chandra Sen of the Brahmo Samaj and Narendranath Datta (1863-1902), who took the name of Vivekananda when he temporarily became a hermit. The latter's powerful personality and charisma attracted great interest in the United States when he attended the Parliament of Religions there in 1892. Afterwards he toured America and England for three years, disseminating Ramakrishna's teaching. Vivekananda stressed that Hinduism was the only religion that recognizes ways to reach divine reality. He established the Ramakrishna Mission which has representatives throughout the world. There is a huge new headquarters at Gol Park, Calcutta. The Mission also carries out charitable work in countries where there are Indian communities.

Another outstanding personality was the Bengali Aurobindo Ghose (1872-1950). He was educated mainly in England. On his return to India in 1893 he entered the State service of Baroda and began to study Indian culture and yoga. The partition of Bengal in 1905 caused him to join the Nationalist movement which culminated in his imprisonment for sedition in 1908. Whilst in gaol Ghose underwent a profound mystical experience. After his release he went to the French settlement of Pondichery where he wrote books and developed his own philosophy of Integral Yoga. From 1920 onwards the actual running of the community was in the hands of a French woman known as 'the Mother' who died a few years ago. She is venerated as much as her *guru*, and her portraits hang in every room of the ashram.

One notable ashram was that of Ramana Maharishi (died 1950) at Tiruvanamalai. He was a man of a sensitive and highly spiritual character whose mystical experiences in imagining the agonies of death raised him to such a state of enlightenment that he seemed no longer of this world. Thenceforth he remained silent, in order to experience consciousness of the One unity underlying multiplicity.

Other so-called *gurus* of a less desirable nature are established in Europe and America, including Bhagwan Sri Rajneesh, the 'free sex' *guru*, who owns three jet planes, twenty-seven Rolls Royces, a cult centre in Suffolk and another in America.

The Theosophical Society

This was founded in New York in 1875 by the mysterious Russian, Madame Helena Petrovna Blavatsky (1831-1891) and Colonel H. S. Olcott. Although founded by Europeans, the Society was welcomed by Hindus who had for so long had their religion misunderstood, ridiculed and denigrated by Christian missionaries. It was decided to open a centre in India and the notable Mrs Annie Besant was sent as leader. She devoted the rest of her life to the welfare of Indians and to expounding the virtues of Hinduism and the basic truths of all religions. She attempted unsuccessfully to introduce a World Teacher into the Society by grooming the young brahmin Krishnamurti (born in 1896) for the office, but in 1929 he announced that he did not want disciples. He left the Society and now travels the world teaching a moderate and unsectarian spirituality. The essence of his teaching is that only through a complete change of heart in the individual can there come about a change in society for good. Krishnamurti is interested in education and has established schools in England and the United States. Another 'defector' from the Society was Rudolf Steiner (1861-1925), the founder of the Anthroposophical Society.

Mrs Besant was a prime mover in nationalist politics, and was elected President of the Congress Party. She also founded the Banaras Central Hindu College in 1898, which later formed the nucleus of the Banaras Hindu University.

Theosophy asserts that there is one Universal Spirit or Absolute manifesting itself in the cosmic processes and in the potentialities of the human spirit. The universe develops cyclically — activities begin, reach their height and then diminish to be followed by a period of quiescence. But the results already achieved are not lost since they remain in germinal form until the unfolding of the next universe. All souls (in this system called Monads), emanate from the Absolute and so are essentially divine but in a state of unawareness, until awakened when they descend into matter. The Monads become successively encased in mineral, vegetal or animal forms.

With the commencement of conscious evolution the law of *karma* simultaneously begins to operate. Good actions promote the unfolding of the individual's spiritual progress, bad actions thwart the fulfilment of the spirit's potentialities. Reincarnation gives time for the spirit to become expert in right action so that ultimately it may fulfil the Divine plan. The Adepts or perfected beings (also called the White Brotherhood or Mahatmas) supervise the world process. They are not only divine but in complete sympathy with mankind and all beings, a view reminiscent of the Mahayana Buddhist *bodhisattva* doctrine.

A special and intimate relationship exists between mankind and animals, who are different from man in degree only. Hence they should never be exploited or cruelly treated, for their relationship with man is intended to be of mutual benefit, since all creatures co-operate in the divine plan which alone gives meaning to existence.

The headquarters of the Theosophical Society is at Adyar, a suburb of Madras. It continues to publish Hindu classics and to encourage the syncretism of all religions.

Mahatma Gandhi

Mohandas Karamchand Gandhi (1869-1948) was born a member of the merchant caste. He regarded himself as an orthodox Hindu although he was much influenced by nineteenth-century European liberalism, the Sermon on the Mount, and the writings of Tolstoy. Although in former times some Indians had opposed caste distinctions and advocated non-violence and the equality of women, their influence was not widespread; whereas Gandhi actually turned Hindu thought towards a more egalitarian social order instead of the exclusive hierarchy of caste. Once, when asked to give the essence of Hinduism, he replied that it was contained in the first verse of the *Isa Upanisad:* 'All this that we see in this great universe is permeated by God/ Renounce it and enjoy it/ Do not covet anybody's wealth or possessions.' The world has to be renounced because as ephemeral beings we can never possess it, but it may be enjoyed as God's creation.

During his youth Gandhi had experienced the distracting and weakening effects of lust and for the rest of his life he was strictly continent. However, this did not turn him against women, among whom he had many good friends, including the English woman Miss Slade who died in Vienna in 1982.

Gandhi really 'lived' his religion. Power and wealth were meaningless to him, his main aim being to attain personal liberation from desire, anger, greed, vanity, etc. The desire for liberation from the British always remained secondary to his personal aim.

Gandhi taught and exemplified the main virtues of non-injury to all creatures, continence, and truth. However, he was well aware that the individual conscience is fallible and therefore emphasized that if it went against non-violence or continence the conscience was faulty, for these two qualities lead inevitably to harmlessness, kindness, restraint in all things, and universal compassion.

Gandhi was careful to retain all that was good in the Hindu tradition. This included the daily religious rites performed by orthodox householders, temple-worship, and the veneration of the cow which so irritates many Europeans (perhaps because of subconscious feelings of guilt at the exploitation of cattle and other animals in the West). Since Vedic times cattle were highly regarded, being the chief source of food and of numerous by-products useful to man. In post-Vedic times cow slaughter was forbidden and this gentle animal came to represent the abundance of nature personified as Surabhi, the cow of plenty. To Gandhi the cow provided so much that India needs, and it also symbolized innocence and the protection of the helpless.

Gandhi lived extremely simply, eating vegetarian food and wearing a homespun cotton loincloth and cloak. He stressed the importance of the spinning wheel, the significance of which was immediately understood by Indians. The loincloth denotes the simple self-sufficient life and the total abnegation of a holy man who reduces his needs to the very basics necessary for life; whilst the spinning wheel signifies Gandhi's care for the destitute. His teaching concerning non-violence was all-important to him and, when the first flowering of non-violence among Hindus and Moslems gave way to the old hatreds and violence, he felt he had failed.

Gandhi never regarded himself as a religious reformer and founded no society or mission, but he and Nehru were the two main architects of Indian independence. However, Gandhi did establish an ashram, a religious community open to men, women and children, which also supported and developed local industries. He will long be remembered for his heroic attempts to alleviate the disabilities suffered by the 'Untouchables' whom he called Harijan, 'sons of God', Hari being a title of Visnu.

Gandhi was strongly opposed to Partition as he realized it would destroy any hope of a united India, as well as causing the deaths of millions of Hindus and Moslems. Ironically, it was Gandhi's brotherly concern for Moslems that caused him to be assassinated by a fanatical member of the extreme Hindu movement called the Mahasabha ('Great Assembly').

Some of Gandhi's ideals are being carried on by Vinoba Bhave who continues to have much success with *bhoodan* (*bhudan*), the giving of land to the landless. Gandhi's ideals are still admired throughout India but they have not been put into practice, although some Western protest movements have latched on to the non-resistance concept.

Appendix A:

A Guide to the Pronunciation of Sanskrit

The long vowels: ā, ī, e, ai, o and au are pronounced as in the following English words: farm, machine, prey, aisle, go and cow respectively.

The short vowels: a, i, u are pronounced as the vowels in cat, bit and bull. Ṛ is classed as a short vowel and is pronounced as 'ri' in rich.

The aspirated consonants th and ph are pronounced as in pothole and shepherd, *never* as in English thin and photo.

C is pronounced as ch in Church. S approximates to English sit, ś and ṣ to sh in shape.

The distinctions between the other sub-dotted 'retroflex' consonants (ṭ, ṭh, ḍ, ḍh, ṇ) and the dentals are not important to the general reader.

Mutations

These occur when a particular terminal vowel of one word coalesces with the initial vowel of the following word. Thus a+a merge and become ā; a+ā become ā as in Śaṅkara and acarya, which become Śaṅkarācārya. A terminal u before an initial a changes to v as in Manu+antara (manvantara). A terminal a followed by an initial u coalesce and become o as in Kaṭha Upaniṣad (Kaṭhopaniṣad).

Appendix B:

Sanskrit Terms and Proper Names

Abhinava Gupta
ācārya
Acyuta
Ādi Samāj
Āditya
Aḍiyar
Ādyaśakti
Āgama
Āgamānta Śaiva
Aghorī
ahaṁkāra
ahiṁsa
Aitareya brāhmaṇa
Ājīvika
Akṣapāda
Ālvār
Āṇḍāl
Aniruddha
anīśvaravāda
aṇu
apāmārga
Appar
apūrva
araṇi
Āraṇyaka
Araṇyānī
Ardhanarīśvara
artha
āsana
aśrama
āśrama
astika
Asunītī
asura
Āsurī
aśvattha
āśvina
ātman
Atri
AUM
avatāra
avidyā
āyurveda
Bāla Kṛṣṇa
Bālarāma
Bālgopāl
Bali
Bānī
Basava
Bhagavadgītā

Bhāgavata
Bhāgavata Purāṇa
Bhairava
Bhairavī
bhakti
bhakti mārga
Bhāskarācārya
Bhatṛhari
Bhava
Bhaviṣya
bhedābheda
Bhīma
Bhīṣma
Bhṛgu
Bhū
bhūdān
bhūta
Bhūtanātha
bīja
bindu
bodhisattva
Brahmā
brahmacārin
Brahmamīmāṁsā
brahman
Brāhmaṇa
brāhmaṇa (a priest)
Brahmāṇḍa
Brahmasūtra
Brāhmo Samāj
Bṛhadāraṇyaka Upaniṣad
buddhi
Caitanya
cakra
Cāmuṇḍā
caṇḍāla
Caṇḍī
Caṇḍikā
Caraka
Cārvāka
Chāndogya Upaniṣad
citta
Dādū
Dādūpanthī
dākinī
Dakṣiṇāmūrti
darśana
Daśaratha
deva
Devakī
Devī
dhāraṇā
dhāraṇī
Dharmaśāstra
Dharmasūtra
Dhātar
Dhiṣaṇā
Dhṛtarāṣṭra
dhyāna
Dhyānabindu Upaniśad
dikpāla
dīksā
dīpāvalī
dolā
Draupadī
dṛṣṭi
Durgā
Dvaitādvaita
dvāpara
Dvārāka
dvāravatī
dvija
ekagrata
Emūṣa
gandharva
Gaṇeśa
Gaṅgā
garbhagṛha
Garuḍa
Gauḍapāda
Gaurī
gāyatrī

Girīśa
Gītāgovinda
gñā
gopī
gopuram
Gorakhnāth
Gorakhnāthī
grāmadevatā
gr̥hastha
Gr̥hyasūtra
guṇa
haṁsa
Hanuman
Hari
Harijan
Harivaṁsa
Haṭha Yoga
Hiraṇyakaśipu
Holī
Hotrā
iccha
Iḍā
Īśa
Īśāna
iṣṭadevatā
Īśvara
Īśvara-Kr̥ṣṇa
īśvaravāda
Itihāsa
Jagannātha
jaṅgama
jāti
Jayadeva
jīva
jīvanmukti
jīvātman
Jñāna Yoga
Jñāneśvara
Kabīr
Kabīrpanthī
kāla
Kālamātā
Kālāmukha
kali (an age of the world)
Kālī
kālīghaṭ
Kalkī or Kalkin
Kalyāṇī
kama
Kāma
Kaṁsa
Kāñcī
Kānphaṭa yogī
Kāpālabhr̥t
Kāpālika
karīṣin
karma
Kārttikeya
Kaśyapa
Kaṭha
Kāthiawār
Kauśitaki
khaṭvāṅga
kravyād
kriya
kriyāśakti
Kr̥ṣṇa
kr̥ta
kṣatriya
Kumārila Bhaṭṭa
Kuṇḍalinī
kūrma
Kurukṣetra
Lakṣmaṇa
Lakṣmī
Lakulīśa
lakuṭa
Laṅkā
līlā
liṅga
Liṅgarāja
Liṅgāyat

loka
Lokāyata
Madhva
Mādhva (cult)
Mahābhārata
mahābhūta
Mahādeva
Mahākāla
Mahā Nārāyaṇa
Mahārāja
Mahāsabhā
mahātma
Mahāvidyā
Mahāvīra
Mahāyāna
Mahāyogī
mahāyuga
Maheśvara
Maithilī
maithuna
makara
mala
māṁsa
manas
Manasā
Mānavadharmaśāstra
maṇḍala
mantra
Manusmṛti
Marāṭha
Marīci
Mārkaṇḍeya
Mathurā
mātṛkā
matsya
māyā
Meykaṇṭar
Mīmāṁsā
Mīnākṣī
mokṣa or mukti
mudrā
Muṇḍaka
muni
nāga
Nakula
Nāmdev
Nandi or Nandin
nara
Nārada
Nāradīya
naraka
Narasiṁha or Nṛsiṁha
Nārāyaṇa
nāstika
Naṭarāja
Nātha
navapatrikā
Navyanyāya
Nāyaṇmār
Nimavāt
Nimbārka
nirguṇa-brahman
Nityānanda
Nyāya
Nyāya-vaiśeṣika
OṂ
padma (lotus)
Padmā
padmāsana
Pañcala
Pāñcarātra
Pāñcarātra āgama
Pāṇḍava
Paṇḍharpur
Pāṇḍu
Parama-Śiva
paramātman
Para Śakti
Paraśurāma
Parikṣit
pariṇāma
Pārvatī

pāśa
paśu
Pāśupata
pati
Pillai Lokācārya
piṇḍa
Piśāca
piśācadruma
pitṛ
Prabhākara
Prahlāda
Prajāpati
prakṛti
prakṛti-puruṣa
pralaya
prāṇapratiṣṭhā
praṇava
prāṇāyāma
Prārthana Samāj
prasāda
Pratyabhijñasūtra
pratyāhāra
Pṛthivī
pūjā
Puṇḍarīka
Puraṁdhi
Purāṇa
puruṣa
Purvamīmāṁsā
puṣṭimārga
Rādhā
Rādhā Soāmī
rāja
Rājadhirāja
rajas
Rājasūya
Rākā
rākṣasas
Rāma
Rāmacandra
Rāmakrishna
Rāmānanda
Rāmānuja
Ramāvat or Rāmāndī (cult)
Rāmāyaṇa
Rāmdās
Rātrī
Rāvaṇa
ṛbhu
Ṛgveda
ṛṣi
ṛta
ṛtu
Rudra
Rukmiṇī
rūpa
śabda
Śabdabrahman
sac-cid-ananda
Sadhu
Sadyojāta
saguṇa
saguṇa-brahman
Sahadeva
Sahajānanda
Sahajiyā
Śaiva
Śaiva Siddhānta
Śākinī
Śākta
Śakti
samādh
samādhi
sāman
samarasya
Sāmaveda
Sāmavidhāna
Sāṁkhya
Sāṁkhyakarika
saṁsāra
samudramathana
saṁyoga

sanātana dharma
Sāṇḍilya
Śaṅkara
Śaṅkarācārya
Saṅkarṣaṇa
saṅnyāsin
saptamatṛkā
Sarasvatī
Śarva
śāstra
Śatapatha brāhmaṇa
sattva guṇa
Sāvitrī
Śeṣa
Siddha
Siddhānta śāstra
Siddhi
Śilpa śāstra
siṁha
Sinivālī
Sītā
Sītālā
Śiva
śivadṛṣṭi
Śivādvaita
Śivājī
Śivajñānabodham
Śivarātrī
Śiva saṁhitā
śivatattva
smṛti
soma
Somānda
śraddhā
śramaṇa
Śrauta sūtra
Śrī
Śrīkaṇṭha
Śrī Vaiṣṇava
śrīvatsa
śrīyantra
sṛṣṭi
śruti
śūdra
Sugrīva
Śulva sūtra
Sundaramūrti
śūnya
Śūnyasaṁpadane
śūnyavāda
Sūrya
Suśruta saṁhitā
sūtra
svāhā
Svāmī Dayānanda Sarasvatī
Svāmi Nārāyaṇa
svaprakāśa
Śvetāsvatāra Upaniṣad
Syamā
Taittirīya
tamas guṇa
tapas
Tatpuruṣa
tattva
tat tvam asi
tīrtha
Tirujñāna-Sambandhar
Trika
trimūrti
triśūla
Tukārām
Ugra
Umā
upanayana
Upaniṣad
Upapurāṇa
Utpāla
Uttaramīmāṁsā
Vāc
Vaḍagalai
vāhana

Vaikhānasasūtra
Vaiśeṣika
vaiṣṇava
vaiśya
Vaitaraṇī
vājapeya
Vajrayāna
Vallabhācārya
Vālmīki
vāmācāra
Vāmadeva
Vāmana
Vana Durgā
Varāha
vārkarī panth
varṇa
Varuṇa
vasana
Vāsudeva
Vāsudeva-Kṛṣṇa
Vasugupta
Vāyu
Vedāṅga
Vedānta
Vedānta Deśika or
  Veṅkaṭanatha
Vedāntasāra
Vedāntasūtra
Veṅkaṭanātha
Veṅkateśvara
vetāla
vibhūti
videhamukti
vidyā
Vidyāpati
vidyātattva
Vijjala
Virajā
Vīraśaiva
Viśiṣṭādvaita
Viṣṇu
viṣṇupaṭṭa
Viśuddhādvaita
Viṭhobā
Viṭṭhala
Vivekānanda
Vṛndāvana or Brindaban
vṛṣṇi
Vṛtra
Vyāsa
vyūha
Yādava
Yājñavalkya
yakṣa
yakṣī
Yama
Yamī
Yamunā
yantra
yātudhāna
yātudhānī
Yogasūtra
yoginī
yoni
Yudhiṣṭhira

Glossary

Ahimsa: Literally, 'non-injury', abstinence from harming any living being.

Ajivika: A movement headed by Makkhali Gosala, a contemporary of the Buddha. It lasted until the medieval period when it was absorbed into the Hindu Pancaratra cult.

Alvars: The twelve notable poet-saints of Tamil vaisnavism who lived between the seventh and tenth centuries AD. Their fervent 'hymns' contributed to the devotional (*bhakti*) type of religion. Nathamuni (in the tenth century), the first teacher of the southern vaisnavas, collected the poems of the Alvars into a scripture called the *Prabandham* or *Nalayiram* ('Four thousand') which attained a similar status to that of the Veda.

Anisvaravada: Literally, the 'non-Lord (Isvara) doctrine', i.e., atheism. Indian atheism rejects the idea of a creator-deity and a personal god, but none the less does not deny intra-cosmic deities.

Apsarases: See *Gandharva*(s).

Aryans: 'Belonging to Ariana or Aria' the eastern part of ancient Persia (Iran). The Sanskrit speaking immigrants into India called themselves *arya*, 'noble' or 'excellent', to distinguish themselves from the aborigines of the country. The Aryans were originally a racial group whose language was the source of a number of related languages: Sanskrit, Old Persian, Greek, Celtic, etc. These groups, speaking Indo-

European languages, had traversed Iran before entering north-west India during the early and middle part of the second millennium BC. In later times the term *arya* was applied to the first of the three castes.

Asana: A yogic posture or mode of sitting, closely associated with breathing techniques (especially those of Hatha Yoga), which control the physiological processes.

Asrama: An ashram or meeting place where followers live and attend their spiritual teacher (*guru*).

Asramas(s): The four stages of an ideal life, which applies primarily to brahmins: the first stage, from initiation until marriage, is that of a celibate student (*brahmacarin*); the second, the period as a householder and head of a family (*grhastha*); the third, when the householder gives up his possessions and lives as a hermit in some solitary place; and the fourth, when as a wandering recluse (*sannyasin*) he lives by begging and attempts to attain final liberation from this world.

Astika: 'Orthodox' teaching. Its literal meaning is 'it is'; unorthodox teaching is termed *nastika* 'it is not'.

Asura: In the Rgveda this term is synonymous with god (*deva*) and is an honorific title applied to Indra and Varuna. From the later Vedic period onwards, it designated evil deities who were at war with the Aryans and perpetually hostile to the gods.

Atman: The eternal principle in living beings; the soul, spirit or self; a key concept in Hinduism. Sometimes it refers to the one Universal Spirit animating the cosmos. In the Advaita Vedanta system *atman* is identified with the impersonal *brahman* or Absolute underlying the apparent, but illusory, plurality of the world. From one point of view the *atman* is present in an individual's secret centre; from another it protects, supports, and gives him his identity. (See *jiva*.)

Avatara: An incarnation; a 'descent' of a deity to earth.

Avidya: 'Ignorance', the opposite of knowledge or spiritual insight into the nature of reality. In most Indian traditions spiritual ignorance lies at the root of mankind's ills.

Ayodhya: See *Mathura*.

Benaras: Also known as Varanasi and Kasi. The most important sacred city and centre of pilgrimage. It is situated on the banks of the Ganges, which is said to lie at the intersection of the celestial Ganges or Milky Way, the terrestrial Ganges, and the invisible underground Ganges. A large area round the city is also sacred and includes many temples and shrines.

Bhakti: Loving devotion to God. The way of devotion (*bhakti-marga*) has been one of the main characteristics of Hinduism since classical times.

Bhakti-marga: See *Bhakti.*

Bhakti-yoga: A yogic method to obtain release by loving devotion to God. It is closely associated with grace (*prasada*). *Bhakti yoga* is a method advocated by Krsna in the *Bhagavadgita.*

Bhuta(s): Evil spirits, ghosts, or demons of lower status than human beings. They include *pisacas, pretas, raksasas,* etc. Many of the indigenes were regarded as demonic by the Aryans.

Bija-mantra: A mystical letter or syllable which forms the essential part of the mantra of a deity.

Brahman: (1). Literally, 'growth', 'expansion', 'development', from the root *brh* 'to increase'. It also means 'sacred power', 'ultimate reality'. Originally *brahman* meant the 'power' implicit in Vedic sacrificial ritual. In the *Upanisads* it denotes the supreme principle which is sometimes conceived impersonally, at other times personally as the Lord Isvara. *Brahman* is the Absolute, the transcendent essence of every form of existence and hence identical with *atman.* It is beyond the categories of name and form and is simultaneously transcendent and immanent.

(2). A class of men or priests (*brahmanas*) who are the repositories and communicators of sacred knowledge. (See *caste.*)

Buddha, The: See *Buddhism.*

Buddhi: 'Intellect', a term derived from the same root as 'enlightenment'. In the Samkhya system it is one of the stages in the evolution of Nature. The main function of the intellect is to reflect on to the mind (*manas*) the light emanating from *atman.*

Buddhism: A major religion which originated in north-east India in the sixth century BC. It is based on the teaching of Gautama (or Gotama) who became the Buddha (the

'Awakened One'). Gautama was the son of a ruler of the Sakya tribe who lived in the Himalayan foothills of what is now Nepal. The Buddha's teaching consists of an analysis of the human situation, the nature and structure of human personality, and the way to overcome all forms of suffering. The interdependence of all creatures is stressed and the need to avoid all extremes. The earlier form of the religion was known as Hinayana or 'Lesser Means' (to liberation) and was atheistic. The later Mahayana or 'Great Means' was theistic. The latter flourished in north-west India and came under the influence of Graeco-Roman culture. Mahayana Buddhism stressed the necessity for compassion for all creatures without exception, as well as the attainment of wisdom, and also inaugurated the *bodhisattva* doctrine. A *bodhisattva* is a spiritually advanced person who gives up his own liberation in order to remain in this world to help all creatures.

Cakra: (1) 'Wheel', 'discus', 'circle'. A symbol of the sun and of cosmic order (*rta*).

(2). In Tantrism the mystical name of the wheels or centres of the subtle body distributed along the spinal column. Various faculties and divinities are said to be present in these centres. By arousing and controlling these forces a *yogin* can gain both physiological control and physical power, and purification leading to liberation.

Candala(s): Outcaste, a person of the lowest of the mixed tribes; especially one born of a *sudra* father and a *brahmin* mother.

Caraka: The author of a first-century book on Indian medicine (*ayurveda*) based on earlier medical works.

Carvaka: A materialistic philosophical school said to have been founded by a man of the same name. It is also called Lokayata — the view that there is no world (*loka*) beyond the empirical cosmos. The Carvaka flourished from about the sixth century BC until the medieval period, when it declined rapidly. The Carvakas were against ritual and were atheistic. They explained consciousness as a property arising out of a particular blend of specific material elements, just as alcohol forms when certain materials are blended.

Caste: The Sanskrit term is *varna*, 'colour'; a more modern term is *jati*. In Vedic times there were said to be four classes of people. The upper three: *brahmanas* (brahmins), *ksatriyas* (warriors and nobles), and *vaisyas* (merchants and agriculturalists), were fully initiated into the Aryan community and known as the 'twice-born' (*dvija*). The fourth class consisted of members of the subjugated population called *sudras.* Theoretically the classes were bound to social functions and specific crafts and trades, somewhat similar to the ancient guilds of Europe. Later, tribal and other groups, including members of unorthodox religious cults such as Jainas, were gradually assimilated. Later still a fifth class, the 'Untouchables', came into existence. One of the best known groups of 'Untouchables' is that of the *candalas* who performed unpleasant and impure tasks. Although foreigners are also 'Untouchables' they were often assimilated to an appropriate caste. Thus the Greek rulers had the status of *ksatriyas.* Strict caste rules are increasingly difficult to follow at the present day, especially in cities, but the caste system does provide a certain amount of welfare for its members. It also provided a framework for diverse social and religious groups to live amicably together.

Citta: Mental activity which yogic techniques aim to arrest.

Darsana: A religio-philosophical system or viewpoint.

Dharana: Perfect yogic concentration (associated with retention of breath) in which the dissolution of the mind occurs.

Dharani(s): Protective spells or mystical verses.

Dharma: 'Law', 'sacred law', 'universal norm', 'custom', 'justice', 'morality', 'duty', 'religion', etc. *Dharma* is a later development of the Vedic *rta*, 'divine law', associated particularly with the correct performance of sacrificial rites. Ontologically, *dharma* represents the immanent dynamic order or inner balance of all cosmic manifestations; in theology it refers to divine law; in epistemology, to validity or truth. *Dharma* is held to be an equivalent of *brahman.* The *Dharmasutras* (composed from about the fifth to the second century BC) deal with conduct; the later *Dharmasastras* are extensive expositions of the *dharma*, the most important being the Laws of Manu (*Manavadharmasastra*, also known as the *Manusmrti*).

Dhyana: 'Meditation' practised in both Hindu and Buddhist schools.

Diksa: 'Initiation'. (See *Dvija*.)

Divali or *dipavali:* 'Festival of lights' in October to November, when Laksmi and Kali are worshipped.

Dola: The 'swing' festival when images of the deity are swung.

Dravidians: The *dravida* speaking peoples of southern India, who contributed greatly to the development of Hinduism. The principal Dravidian languages are: Tamil, Canarese (or Kannada), Telugu, and Malayalam; these may be related distantly to the Finno-Ugrian group of languages.

Drsti: Literally, 'seeing' or 'viewing'; a philosophical viewpoint or system.

Durga puja: 'Worship (*puja*) of Durga'. An autumn festival in Bengal, the tenth night of which is the most important, when the Rama play (*Ramalila*) is performed.

Dvaravati or *Dwarka:* See *Mathura*.

Dvija: 'Twice-born'. A ceremony in which a *guru* initiates (*diksa*) a boy into one of the three upper castes. The ceremony usually takes place between the ages of eight to twelve when the boy is invested with the sacred thread which is worn over the left shoulder and under the right arm.

In Tantrism and Saivism a devotee is 'reborn' after initiation and introduced to secret knowledge that aids him on his way to liberation.

Ekagrata: One-pointed concentration achieved by means of breath control and sense withdrawal from external stimuli, in preparation for the attainment of *dharana*.

Gandharva(s): Male celestial musicians of the gods. The nymph-like Apsarases are their female counterparts.

Garbhagrha: The small, central, windowless room in a temple that houses the image of the deity to whom the temple is dedicated.

Gayatri or *Savitri:* A short prayer or mantra addressed to the sun (Savitar): 'We meditate on that excellent light of the divine Sun: May it illuminate our minds'. It is repeated daily by every 'twice-born' man at his morning and evening devotions. The *gayatri* is personified as a goddess, the wife of Brahma.

Gopi(s): The cow-herd girls among whom Krsna spent his idyllic childhood.

Gramadevata(s): Local or village deities.

Guna(s): The three inseparable constituents or qualities

comprising Nature: *sattva*, 'essence', 'truth', 'goodness'; *rajas*, 'energy', 'action', 'passion'; and *tamas*, 'mass', 'inertia', 'darkness'. When the three *gunas* are perfectly balanced, manifestation cannot take place; but when the equilibrium is disturbed, the interplay of the *gunas* brings about the evolution of Nature and creation occurs. Every being has one or other of the *gunas* predominant in its character.

Guru: A teacher of religious knowledge and yogic techniques. The primary meaning of the term is 'heavy', suggesting weighty with vast knowledge.

Hamsa: 'Goose'. The wild goose (*Anser indicus*) which breeds on the lakes of Central Asia and migrates in winter to all parts of India. In Vedic lore the goose was closely associated with the sun and represented the male principle of fertility. Because of its whiteness, beauty and elegance in flight it symbolized the One Spirit (*atman*), as it is equally at home on land, on the waters, and in the sky. Later it symbolized the individual spirit condemned to transmigrate from body to body during the long series of rebirths and redeaths. It also represents knowledge and hence is the mount of Brahma and his consort Sarasvati; its lofty flight is likened to the spiritual efforts of the devout Hindu to attain *brahman*.

Hatha-yoga: The employment of physical energy as a means to achieve liberation.

Hiranyagarbha: 'Golden embryo'. Brahma (or Prajapati) impregnated the primeval waters and manifested himself as a golden embryo out of which the cosmos developed.

Holi: A spring festival originally connected with the god of love, Kama. At this time caste and other social prohibitions are ignored.

Istadevata: The 'chosen deity' through which a person or group approaches ultimate reality; thus no specific deity is ever regarded as unique.

Isvara: Literally, 'Lord', 'prince'. A term applied to God as a personal being and supreme object of worship, but he is not necessarily a creator. In the Advaita Vedanta system, *brahman* is without qualities or attributes when viewed from the standpoint of higher truth, but from the mundane level *brahman* is a personal deity with qualities. (See *sagunam brahman*.)

Isvaravada: 'Theism'; belief in a supreme Lord or God. It does not exclude belief in other gods regarded as subordinate to the supreme deity.

Itihasa: Various works which include the Epics, Puranas and Law Books of Manu that form part of the auxiliary canon of orthodox Hinduism supplementing the Veda.

Jaina: A follower of Jainism.

Jainism: A major religion of great antiquity. Formerly Western Indologists regarded Mahavira (sixth century BC) as the founder, but he now appears to have been a teacher or reformer of a much earlier tradition.

The first centre of influence was the Ganges region; but in the third century BC a severe famine forced many Jainas to migrate to the Deccan. Henceforth Jainism became established in the south and west of India. A schism occurred at this time which gave rise to the Svetambaras and the Digambaras. This was mainly concerned with whether or not monks should practise nudity, which was a sign that they had renounced the world. Other than this the two sects differ little in their tenets.

As well as the teaching of strict harmlessness, self-mortification and asceticism are highly valued as a means to remove the accumulated *karma* affecting every being. However, this method is only practicable for monks; the laity support the monks and endeavour to live up to the ascetic ideal as far as possible. Jainism is an atheistic system, although a hierarchy of gods inhabiting the cosmos is recognized. The universe is vast and eternal and is understood to include heavens and innumerable hells. When liberation is attained, the individual life-monad is removed forever from the long series of rebirths.

Despite Jainism's great antiquity it predicts a gradual decline and eventual disappearance of the religion in the present age, but it will be renewed when the next cycle of history commences.

Jainism is one of the three 'heterodox' Indian systems which deny the validity of the Veda as an infallible source of knowledge.

Japa: A devotional exercise consisting in muttering prayers or repeating a mantra or name of a deity. The best *japa* is when the prayer is simply 'thought';

Jati: 'Birth'. (See *Caste*.)

Jiva or *jivatman:* The empirical self or soul when embodied. The Advaita Vedanta system states that the empirical self is ultimately unreal but is implicated in the series of rebirths. Liberation comes with the realization of the identity of the self and *brahman.*

Jivanmukti: 'Living release'. One who has attained release in this life, and who at death will never again be reborn.

Jnana-yoga: A method of achieving liberation principally by pursuit of intellectual knowledge.

Kaivalya: 'Isolation': Literally, 'wholeness', 'completeness'. It is the state of liberation reached by yogic means whereby the soul becomes isolated from the psycho-physical organism, from the world and from other souls.

Kali-yuga: The fourth and final period of cosmic development. We are now in the period of the 'iron age' which immediately precedes the dissolution of the universe.

Kalpa: A vast period of time constituting the duration of the world and lasting 4,320 million terrestrial years of mortals. This period corresponds to a 'day' of Brahma's life. At the end of the age the universe dissolves into non-manifestation during the 'night of Brahma'.

Kama: 'Desire', 'love'. Yogic techniques aim to eliminate it so that the *atman* can be reabsorbed ultimately by *brahman.*

Kanci: See *Mathura.*

Karma or *karman:* 'Act', 'works', 'action'. The inexorable law which controls rebirth. *Karman* also includes ritual and ethical action as enjoined in the Vedas. Every act produces an effect which leaves behind a psychic residue (also called *karman*) which binds the soul to the world of existence. (See *Vasana.*)

Karma-yoga: The 'way (*marga*) of good works'. A yogic technique designed to achieve liberation through altruistic action.

Ksatriya: A member of the warrior and noble class, the second of the four main castes.

Kundalini: 'Coiled'. A mythical serpent symbolizing the cosmic power (*sakti*) existing in every living being.

Linga or *lingam:* 'Phallus', 'sign'. A symbol of Siva's power over nature and all living beings.

Lokayata: See *Carvaka.*

Mahayana Buddhism: See *Buddhism.*

Mahayuga(s): See *Yugas.*

Makara: A mythical aquatic animal which represents the unmanifested state of the cosmos. It is the mount or vehicle (*vahana*) of Varuna and Ganga.

Makara(s): The so-called 'Five M's': alcohol, meat, fish, symbolic gestures, and ritual sexual intercourse. The Sanskrit names of these things all begin with 'm'.

Mala(s): 'Impurities' that prevent the soul gaining liberation according to Saiva teaching.

Manas: 'Mind'. In Indian belief mind is a kind of internal organ which co-ordinates material presented by the other senses.

Mandala: See *yantra.*

Mantra: A secret ritual formula given by a *guru* to his pupil during initiation; a sacred formula addressed to a deity; a mystical verse (sometimes personified); or an incantation. Mantras are used by Saktas to acquire supranormal powers. There are seventy million primary mantras and countless secondary ones. The supreme mantra is *OM* which represents the whole of Hindu ideology in condensed form.

Manusmrti or *Manavadharmasastra:* Name of the Law Book of Manu.

Mathura: One of the seven sacred cities of India. They are: Benaras (Kasi), Mathura, Ayodhya, Maya (Hardwar), Kanci (Conjeeveram), and Dvaravati (Dwarka). Mathura is now called Muttra and is situated on the right bank of the Yamuna or Jumna river. It is venerated as the birthplace of Krsna.

Maya: Literally 'measure', reflecting the work of the cosmic architect Visvakarman who 'measured out' the world. *Maya* also means extraordinary or supranormal power; in the Vedanta systems, it refers to cosmic illusion; in Saivism, it is one of the bonds (*pasas*) entangling the soul; in Vaisnavism, it is one of the nine energies (*saktis*) of Visnu. It is sometimes personified as a goddess and identified with Durga.

Moksa or *mukti:* Liberation from the series of rebirths and redeaths.

Muni: 'Sage', 'seer', 'ascetic', 'recluse', especially a holy man who has taken a vow of silence.

Naga(s): (1) Serpent deities inhabiting the waters and the beautiful subterranean city of Bhogavati. They have human faces and serpentine lower extremities.

(2) The tribal Nagas of north-east Assam include: the Garo (Assam); the Ho of the Chota Nagpur plateau; the Bhils (Rajasthan); the Gond and Bhumia (Madhya Pradesh); the Thakurs (Maharashtra); the Mer (Gujarat); the Saora (Orissa); the Chenchu (Andhra Pradesh); the Toda (Nilgiri Hills, Madras); and the Kadar (Cochin, Madras).

Naraka(s): 'Purgatories' rather than hells because, with the exception of the Madhva school, souls are not thought to reside eternally in hell as it is possible for them eventually to attain liberation.

The seven regions of the *narakas* are under the seven regions of Patala, the sphere of various spirits. Living beings move in and out of these regions according to their *karma*.

Nastika: 'Atheistic', a term designating unorthodox schools in the Hindu Tradition. Some Hindu philosophical systems reject the idea of a creator without denying the existence of gods and other supernatural beings in the cosmos.

Nirgunam brahman: 'Without attributes' or qualities; said of the Supreme Being, that is the Absolute, the indefinable ultimate reality which is necessarily devoid of attributes, form or qualities. (See *Sagunam brahman.*)

Nyaya: Originally an atheistic system which later became theistic.

OM: Also called *pranava*. The most important *bija-mantra* that is a sign or manifestation of *brahman* as sound. It is made up of three sounds, *A-U-M*. In Sanskrit o is a diphthong contracted from a and u, which, when pronounced quickly, have the sound of o and, when combined with *m*, give rise to a resonant humming sound which mystically encompasses the past, present and future and all that exists beyond time. Its three constituents represent Brahma, Visnu and Siva, the Hindu triad (*trimurti*).

Padma: 'Lotus'. A symbol of the sun, of purity, of perfection, and of the material aspect of creation. The petals represent creation in its consecutive forms; the open lotus flower denotes the manifested universe. It is also a term for the centres (*cakras*) of the subtle body.

Padmasana: 'Lotus position', one of the most usual meditational postures.

Parinama: The 'evolution' of a thing already existing into a state where other new properties are manifested.

Prakrti: 'Nature', 'matter', as opposed to spirit (*purusa*). *Prakrti* is the substratum of the material world which, according to the Samkhya system, evolves into the countless forms of the world.

Pralaya: 'Dissolution' or dissolving of the world into non-manifestation at the end of the age.

Prana: 'Vital breath'.

Pranava: See *OM*.

Prasada: 'Grace' given by the Lord to his devotees.

Pratyahara: Withdrawal of the senses from external stimuli, constituting the fifth stage of yoga.

Purusa: (1) Literally, 'person', 'man', and by extension 'soul' or 'spirit'. The eternal element in living beings.

(2) The cosmic man (*purusa*) represents inert nature. In one cosmic myth he was offered up by the creating gods as a sacrificial victim. After ritual dismemberment, his death gives birth to the world, its constituent parts being drawn from his substance.

Rajas: The second of the three *gunas*. It imparts energy and motion to the entities in which it predominates. The other *gunas* are *sattva* and *tamas*.

Raja-yoga: 'Royal' yoga as opposed to ancillary methods such as *bhakti-yoga*, etc.

Rsi: A Vedic-inspired sage or seer, a singer of hymns. One of the legendary personages to whom the Hindu texts are revealed. The term *rsi* is sometimes applied honorifically to notable modern persons claiming special insight into divine reality. Originally there were seven legendary *rsis* who, in later works, are regarded as heroes and 'patriarchs' representing the spirit of the mythical period. Metaphorically, the seven *rsis* stand for the seven senses or the seven vital airs of the body.

Rtu or *rta:* 'Fixed time', especially for sacrifices and other regular forms of worship; order; rule; custom. This Vedic term developed into the notion of *dharma* in classical Hinduism.

Rupa: 'Form' or 'image'.

Sac-cid-ananda: 'Being — consciousness — joy', a description of the essence of *brahman*.

Sadhu: A 'holy man', one who has renounced the world to follow the path leading to the Absolute.

Sagunam brahman: Brahman regarded as having qualities; but from the level of higher truth *brahman* is without qualities, attributes, etc. (See *Nirgunam brahman.*)

Sakti: 'Power', 'divine energy' of deities; in men it takes the form of *kundalini.*

Samadhi: The last stage of yoga, culminating in a rapt state of concentration.

Samkhya: One of the six orthodox philosophical systems. It is dualistic and derives from yogic mysticism. Its cosmology was adopted by a number of other movements.

Samsara: Empirical existence and the series of rebirths and redeaths undergone by all beings.

Sastra: See *Sutra(s).*

Sattva: 'Brightness', one of the three *gunas* or constituents of Nature (*prakrti*), which has the property of light, intelligence, truth.

Siddha(s): 'Perfected ones'; semi-divine persons who have achieved *siddhi* (perfection or the complete attainment of any object) which gives supranormal powers.

Siddhi(s): See *Siddha(s).*

Smrti: 'Memory', referring to those writings which are remembered, to distinguish them from 'what is heard', that is Vedic revelation (*sruti*) 'seen' by the early *rsis.*

Sramana: A holy man and wandering ascetic who also may be a religious teacher.

Srautasutras: Works concerned with Vedic ritual.

Srsti: 'Production', 'creation' of the world; emanation. The cosmos is believed to be beginningless and endless, evolving and devolving indefinitely over vast periods of time. Creation out of nothing is not promulgated by any Indian system.

Sruti: See *Smrti.*

Sudra: 'Servant'. A member of the fourth caste.

Sutra(s): Aphoristic expositions concerning ritual observances, family customs, law, etc. Expanded works on the *Sutras* are called *Sastras.*

Svaprakasa: 'Self-luminous Spirit'. In the Advaita Vedanta system the One Self (i.e. *brahman*) manifests itself in all experience. Not being an object of knowledge it can only be known intuitively.

Tad: 'That', a metaphysical term for *atman/brahman.*

Tamas: One of the three *gunas* that represents darkness, mass, dullness and inertia.

Tapas: Literally, 'heat', especially the heat generated by ascetic practices. *Tapas* is both the source of power and the means of gaining it. It refers to an inner fire which corresponds to the outer significance of the god of fire, Agni. This reflects the tendency from the Upanisadic period to correlate microcosm and macrocosm in the Yoga systems.

Tat tvam asi: 'That thou art'. A phrase used as a mantra representing the basic identity of the macrocosm and microcosm. *Tat* (that) represents *brahman*, the universal principal; *tvam* (thou), the *atman*, the individualized and subjective aspect of *brahman.* But widening the idea of the self to include the All precludes the notion of a subject, which implies limitation. Therefore, the supremely moral man identifies his 'self' with the 'self' of all other beings and henceforward delights in their welfare.

Tirtha: 'Sacred place'; a place of pilgrimage usually situated on a river bank where people gather for ritual bathing.

Trimurti: 'Having three forms or aspects'. The view that God was threefold was postulated in classical Hinduism. The *trimurti* consists of: Brahma (creator), Visnu (preserver), and Siva (destroyer). These three aspects of the Divine Being are also identified with the three *gunas.*

Upanayana: An initiation ceremony undergone by all high caste Hindu males at about seven years of age.

Vaisnava: Relating to Visnu or a follower of his cult.

Vaisesika: One of the six orthodox philosophical systems.

Vaisya: See *caste.*

Vamacara: The so-called 'left-hand' forms of Tantrism that involve the breaking of social prohibitions and conventions under ritual conditions, including indulging in the 'Five M's' (*makaras*): alcohol (*madya*); meat (*mamsa*); fish (*matsya*); symbolic gestures (*mudra*, a term that also refers to a female partner); and sexual intercourse (*maithuna*). Sexual symbolism is much used in Tantrism where it represents the reintegration of primordial polarity, the source of the world of multiplicity.

Varna: 'Colour', used to denote the three broad functions among which the castes (*jatis*) are divided.

Vasana: 'Impregnation', the residual trace left by any thought or act; a cause of spiritual ignorance (*avidya*) that produces alienation.

Veda, The: Literally 'knowledge', especially the sacred knowledge handed down orally and which is the basis of the first period of Hinduism. The earliest collection consisted of the *Rgveda, Samaveda* and *Yajurveda.* Later the *Atharvaveda* was added. Other expository works were also included: the *Brahmanas, Aranyakas* and *Upanisads.* Each of the four Vedas has two parts: the *mantra* or words of prayer addressed to the sun and other deities; and the *brahmana* part containing directions for the performance of ceremonies at which the *mantras* are used.

Vedangas: 'Limbs of the Veda', i.e., sciences subsidiary to the veda which include sacrificial techniques, phonetics, prosody, etymology, grammar and astrology.

Vedanta: Philosophical systems which include Advaita Vedanta, Dvaita Vedanta, etc.

Vibhuti: (1) Miraculous powers synonymous with *siddhis* which are especially attributed to Siva, but which may be attained by advanced yogins.

(2) Sacred 'ashes' with which Siva smeared his body. Great powers are attributed to ashes: the power to resurrect the dead, to avert evil, and to bestow fertility.

Vidya or *jnana:* 'Knowledge' or spiritual 'insight' as opposed to *avidya* spiritual darkness or ignorance.

Vira: (1) 'Hero'. An epithet applied to Vedic gods like Indra and the solar Visnu; and to any eminent *siddha* who has overcome all earthly impediments by *tapas* (austerity).

(2) A Tantric adept who had reached the second of the three dispositions, that is the heroic (*virabhava*).

Vrndavana or *Brindaban:* The scene of Krsna's activities and consequently an important place of pilgrimage for vaisnavas.

Yaksa: A collective name for the mysterious vegetal godlings or sprites of rural communities. Their worship stems from pre-Vedic times. *Yaksas* are also included in Jain and Buddhist mythology.

Yama: (1) The judge and ruler of the dead.

(2) The act of restraining or curbing; the first stage of yoga in which the novice endeavours to overcome the distractions of worldly things.

Yantra: A geometric figure representing a deity, power or an element in the universe that will give one power over, or identification with, the deity, etc. A *yantra* is used as a 'chart' or 'instrument' to stimulate 'inner visualization' or meditation. Each deity has its own *yantra* and resides in it during ritual worship.

Yoga: (1) 'Yoking' or 'harnessing'. One of the six orthodox schools of philosophy. It was originally an atheistic system, but later became theistic.

(2) Specific techniques to 'harness' and so control one's physical and mental powers.

Yogi or *yogin:* A follower of the yoga system.

Yogini: A kind of witch associated with Siva and Durga.

Yoni: 'Vulva' or female generative organ depicted as a circular object with a hole in the centre. The *yoni* is the counterpart of the *linga*. When united they symbolize divine procreative energy.

Yuga(s): 'Ages'. Each of the seventy-one *mahayugas* (consisting of 4,320,000 years) are divided into four *yugas:* the *krta* or *satya*, *treta*, *dvapara*, and *kali* of diminishing lengths. Each age is accompanied by the physical and moral degeneration of man. We are now in the *kali* age, the most degenerate of the four. It began at midnight between 17 and 18 February 3102 BC.

References

Chapter 1

1. Majumdar (ed.), *History and Culture of the Indian People*, I. p.361.
2. Stutley, *A Dictionary of Hinduism*, p.100.
3. Winternitz, *History of Indian Literature*, I. pt.1. p.68.
4. Heimann, *Indian and Western Philosophy*, p.34.
5. Gonda, *Visnuism and Sivaism*, p.7.
6. Eliade, *A History of Religious Ideas*, I. p.205.
7. Winternitz, op. cit. i. pt.1, pp.87f.
8. Brockington, *The Sacred Thread*, p.21.
9. Winternitz, I. pt.1. p.105.
10. Winternitz, I. pt.1. p.118.
11. Winternitz, I. pt.1. p.215.
12. Heimann, *Facets of Indian Thought*, pp.90f.
13. Winternitz, I. pt.1, p.266.
14. Ibid., p.240.

Chapter 7

1. Danielou, *Yoga: the Method of Re-Integration*, p.22.
2. Chatterjee and Datta, *Introduction to Indian Philosophy*, Calcutta, 1960, p.295.

Chapter 9

1. Tantric yogic views are found in the *Yogadarsana Upanisad* tr. J. Varenne in *Yoga*, pp.200-222, Chicago, 1976.

2. Varenne, *Yoga*, p.166.
3. Avalon, *Serpent Power*, p.242.
4. Danielou, *Yoga: the Method of Re-integration*, p.76.

Chapter 10

1. *L'Inde classique*, p.323.
2. Danielou, *Hindu Polytheism*, p.155.
3. Bowes, *The Hindu Religious Tradition*, p.227.
4. Majumdar (ed.), *History and Culture of the Indian People*, III, p.419.
5. Kennedy, *The Caitanya Movement*, Calcutta, 1925, pp.17ff.

Chapter 11

1. D. H. H. Ingalls, 'Cynics and Pasupatas. The Seeking of Dishonour', *Harvard Theological Review* LV. Curiously enough T. E. Lawrence also desired to be despised. He wrote to Charlotte Shaw: 'I long for people to look down on me and despise me, and I'm too shy to take the filthy steps which would publicly shame me and put me into their contempt.' 'Death of a Hero' in *Unsolved*, vol. 2, no. 16, p.322, 1984.
2. Brockington, *The Sacred Thread*, p.122.
3. Gonda, *Eye and Gaze in the Veda*, pp.54ff.
4. Eliade, *Yoga: Immortality and Freedom*, pp.306f.
5. Ibid., p.304.

Chapter 12

1. Margaret Hebblethwaite, *Motherhood of God*, 1984. Recently a sculptured female figure (called Christa) on a cross was exhibited in an American church but was hastily removed after an outcry by church members. The *Daily Telegraph* (23.5.84) reports that the Church of Scotland has rejected the idea of 'God as Mother'.
2. *Visnuism and Saivism*, 1970, pp.55, 61.

Chapter 13

1. Eliade, *Yoga: Immortality and Freedom*, p.202.

Chapter 14

1. For more information see my *Illustrated Dictionary of Hindu Iconography*.

2. Zimmer, *Myths*, p.70 and see p.146. Lannoy, *The Speaking Tree*, p.188, suggests that animal mounts are probably totemic.

Bibliography

Chapter 1

Georges Dumezil, *Mitra-Varuna: essai sur deux representations indo-européennes de la souveraineté*, Paris, 1940.

J. Eggeling (tr), *The Satapatha Brahmana*, 5 vols, Sacred Books of the East, Oxford, 1882-1900, reprinted Delhi, 1966.

W. A. Fairservis, *The Roots of Ancient India: the Archaeology of Early Indian Civilization*, 2nd edn. L. 1975.

F. Geldner, *Der Rig-veda*, 3 vols, Cambridge, Massachusetts, 1951.

Jan Gonda, *Vedic Literature (Samhitas and Brahmanas)*, Wiesbaden, 1975.

R. T. H. Griffith, *The Rig-Veda*, 2 vols, Benares, 1896-7, reprint, 1963.

—— *The Texts of the White Yajurveda*, Benares, 1927.

—— *The Hymns of the Samaveda*, Varanasi, 1963.

R. A. Hume, *Thirteen Principal Upanisads*, Oxford, 1921.

Raimondo Panikkar, *The Vedic Experience: Mantramanjari*, L. 1977.

Sten Rodhe, *Deliver us from Evil: Studies on the Vedic Ideas of Salvation*, Lund, 1946.

Chapter 2

Vinoba Bhave, *Talks on the Gita*, 1960.

R. C. Dutt (tr), *The Mahabharata and Ramayana* (abridged edition).

F. Edgerton *et al* have edited a critical edition of the *Mahabharata.*

W. D. P. Hill, *The Holy Lake of the Acts of Rama*, 1952.

P. C. Roy (tr), *The Mahabharata*, Calcutta, 1919-1935.

H. P. Shastri (tr), *The Ramayana of Valmiki*, 3 vols, 1952-9.

R. C. Zaehner, *The Bhagavadgita*, Oxford, 1969.

Chapter 3

E. Burnouf *et al*, *Bhagavata Purana*, 5 vols, Paris, 1840-98.

S. N. Dasgupta, *History of Indian Philosophy*, vol. 3, 1940.

C. Dimmitt and J. A. B. Buitenen, *Classical Hindu Mythology, a reader in the Sanskrit Puranas*, Philadelphia, 1978.

R. C. Hazra, *Studies in the Upapuranas*, 1958.

The Linga Purana, translated by a board of scholars, 2 parts, Delhi, 1973.

The Siva Purana, translated by a board of scholars, 4 vols, Delhi, 1970.

H. H. Wilson, *The Visnu Purana*, 5 vols in 1, 1961.

Chapter 7

Bhattacharyya, *Studies in Nyaya-Vaisesika Theism*, Calcutta, 1961.

Pratima, Bowes, *The Hindu Religious Tradition, a Philosophical Approach*, 1978.

van Buitenen (ed. and tr.), Ramanuja's *Vedarthasamgraha*, 1957.

Surendranath, Dasgupta, *A History of Indian Philosophy*, 5 vols, 1922ff.

Eliot Deutsch, *Advaita Vedanta: a Philosophical Reconstruction*, Honolulu, 1969.

Franklin Edgerton, *The Beginnings of Indian Philosophy*, 1965.

Mircea, Eliade, *Yoga: Immortality and Freedom*, 1958.

Georg Feuerstein (tr), *The Yogasutras of Patanjali*, 1979.

Erich, Frauwallner, *History of Indian Philosophy*, (tr) V. M. Bedekar, Delhi, 1970.

H. von Glasenapp, *Doctrines of Vallabhacharya*, 1959.

Jan Gonda, *Notes on Brahman*, Utrecht, 1950.

E. H. Johnson, *Early Samkhya*, 1937.

A. B. Keith, *Indian Logic and Atomism*, 1921.

—— *The Samkhya System*, 2nd edn. 1949.

G. J. Larson, *Classical Samkhya: an interpretation of its History and Meaning,* Delhi, 1969.
B. K. Matilal, *Nyaya-Vaisesika,* Wiesbaden, 1977.
U. Mishra, *Vedanta School of Nimbarka,* 1940.
S. Radhakrishnan, *The Brahma Sutra,* L. 1960.
P. N. Rao, *The Schools of Vedanta,* Bombay.
B. N. K. Sharma, *A History of Dvaita School of Vedanta,* 2 vols, 1960ff.
S. Singh, *Vedanta Desika: His Life, Works and Philosophy,* 1958.
J. Sinha, *Indian Realism,* 1938.
N. Smart, *Doctrine and Argument in Indian Philosophy,* 1964.
S. M. Srinivasa Chari, *Advaita and Visistadvaita,* 1961.
G. Thibaut, *The Vedanta Sutras, with the Commentary of Ramanuja,* Madras, 1962.
Jean, Varenne, *Yoga and the Hindu Tradition,* (tr) D. Coltman, Chicago, 1976.
Vidyabhusana, S. C., *A History of Indian Logic,* 1921.
Karel, Werner, *Yoga and Indian Philosophy,* Delhi, 1977.

Chapter 9

Agehananda Bharati, *The Tantric Tradition,* 1965.
Mircea Eliade, *Yoga: Immortality and Freedom,* tr. by W. R. Trask, 1958.
Georg Feuerstein (tr), *The Yogasutra of Patanjali,* L. 1979.
Jean Varenne, *Yoga and the Hindu Tradition,* (tr) D. Coltman, Chicago, 1976.
Karel Werner, *Yoga and Indian Philosophy,* Delhi, 1977.
Sir John Woodroffe (nom-de-plume Arthur Avalon), *The Principles of Tantra,* 2 vols, 1914ff. reprint 1952.
—— *The Serpent Power,* 3rd edn, Madras, 1931.

Chapter 10

P. Barz, *The Bhakti Sect of Vallabhacarya,* Faridabad, 1976.
Deben Bhattacharya (tr), *Songs of Krsna,* New York, 1978.
K. E. Bryant, *Poems to the Child-god: structures and strategies in the poetry of Surdas,* Berkeley, 1978.
G. A. Deleury, *The Cult of Vithoba,* Poona, 1960.
E. C. Dimock, *The place of the Hidden Moon: Erotic Mysticism* in the Vaisnava-Sahajiya Cult of Bengal, L. 1966.
H. von Glasenapp, *Doctrines of Vallabhacharya,* 1959.

J. Gonda, *Visnuism and Sivaism, A Comparison*, 1970.
—— *Aspects of Early Visnuism*, 1954.
F. Hardy, *Viraha-Bhakti: The Early History of Krsna Devotion in South India*, Oxford, 1983.
W. D. P. Hill, *The Holy Lake of the Acts of Rama* (an English translation of Tulsi Das' Ramacaritamanasa), Bombay, 1952.
F. E. Keay, *Kabir and His Followers*, 1931.
W. H. McLeod, *Guru Nanak and the Sikh Religion*, Oxford, 1968.
B. S. Miller (tr), *Love Songs of the Dark Lord: Jayadeva's Gitagovinda*, New York, 1977.
U. Mishra, *Vedanta School of Nimbarka*, 1940.
G. A. Nateson (ed), *Ramananda to Ram Tirtha: Lives of the Saints of Northern India*, 1947.
W. G. Orr, *A Sixteenth Century Indian Mystic* [Dadu], 1947.
—— *Kabir*, Oxford, 1974.
B. N. K. Sharma, *History of the Dvaita School of Vedanta*, 2 vols. 1960-1.
—— *Madhva's Teachings in his own Words*, 1963.
S. Singh, *Vedanta Desika: His Life, Works and Philosophy*, 1958.
Ch. Vaudeville, *Etude sur les sources et la composition du Ramayana de Tulsi-Das*, Paris, 1955.

Chapter 11

S. B. Dasgupta, *Obscure Religious Cults as Background to Bengali Literature*, 1946.
P. B. Desai, *Basavesvara and his Times*, Dharwar, 1968.
M. Dhavamony, *The Love of God according to Saiva Siddhanta*, Oxford, 1971.
S. M. Hunashal, *The Lingayat Movement: A Social Revolution in Karnatak*, 1947.
D. H. Lorenzen, *The Kapalikas and Kalamukhas. Two lost Saivite Sects*, New Delhi, 1972.
T. M. P. Mahadevan, *The Idea of God in Saiva-Siddhanta*, 1955.
G. Matthews, *Sivananabodham of Meykanda*, 1948.
S. C. Nandimath, *Handbook of Virasaivism*, Dharwar, 1942.
V. Paranjoti, *Saiva Siddhanta*, 1954.
V. S. Pathak, *History of Saiva Cults in Northern India from Inscriptions*, Varanasi, 1960.

A. K. Ramanujan (tr), *Speaking of Siva*, Harmondsworth, 1973.

L. Renou and J. Filliozat, *L'Inde classique*, I. Paris, 1947-53.

D. Shastri, 'The Lokayatikas and the Kapalikas', *Indian Historical Quarterly*, vii. 1931.

S. Shivapadasundaram, *Shaiva School of Hinduism*, Madras, 1934.

Mohan Singh, *Gorakhnath and Medieval Hindu Mysticism*, 1937.

K. V. Zvelebil, *The Smile of Murugan: on Tamil Literature of South India*, Leiden, 1973.

Chapter 12

Arthur Avalon (Sir John Woodroffe), *Shakti and Shakta*, 1920.

W. G. Beane, *Myth, Cult and Symbols in Sakti Hinduism*, Leiden, 1977.

Agehananda Bharati, *The Tantric Tradition*, 1965.

Goudrian, *et al*, *Hindu Tantric and Sakta Literature*, A History of Indian Literature, II. Fasc. 2, Wiesbaden, 1981.

H. Whitehead, *The Village Gods of South India*, 1921.

Chapter 13

A. Bharati, *The Tantric Tradition*, L. 1965.

S. Gupta *et. al.*, *Hindu Tantrism*, Leiden, 1979.

P. S. Rawson, *The Art of Tantra*, L. 1973.

Jean Varenne, *Le tantrisme: la sexualité transcendée*, Paris, 1977.

Sir John Woodroffe (nom-de-plume Arthur Avalon), *Principles of Tantra*, 2 vols. 1914-16; reprint Madras 1952.

—— *Shakti and Shakta*, 1929; reprint Madras 1969.

—— *Hymns to the Goddess*, 2nd edn. Madras, 1953.

Chapter 14

J. N. Banerjea, *The Development of Hindu Iconography*, 2nd edn. revised and enlarged, Calcutta, 1956.

S. Kramrisch, *The Art of India through the Ages*, 1954.

M. Stutley, *An Illustrated Dictionary of Hindu Iconography*, 1985.

Chapter 15

Anne-Marie Gaston, *Siva in Dance, Myth and Iconography*, Oxford, 1982.

Stella Kramrisch, *The Hindu Temple*, 2 vols. Calcutta, 1946.
George Michell, *The Hindu Temple. An Introduction to its Meaning and Forms*, 1977.
Benjamin Rowland, *The Art and Architecture of India*, 1953.
Andreas Volwahsen, *Living Architecture: Indian*, 1969.

Chapter 17

L. A. Babb, *The Divine Hierarchy: Popular Hinduism in Central India*, New York, 1975.
S. M. Bhardwaj, *Hindu Places of Pilgrimage in India*, L. 1973.
B. Bhattacharyya (ed), *The Cultural Heritage of India*, vol. 4., 1956.
A. C. Mukerji, *Ancient Indian Fasts and Feasts*, 1932.

Chapter 18

Annie Besant, *Annie Besant: An Autobiography*, 1908.
K. W. Bolle, *The Persistence of Religion: an essay on Tantrism and Sri Aurobindo's Philosophy*, Leiden, 1965.
D. M. Datta, *The Philosophy of Mahatma Gandhi*, 1953.
Swami Gambhirananda, *History of the Ramakrishna Math and Mission*, 1957.
M. K. Gandhi, *An Autobiography: or the Story of my Experiments with Truth*, 1959.
M. Gupta (ed), *The Gospel of Sri Ramakrishna*, 1947.
C. H. Heimsath, *Indian Nationalism and Hindu Social Reform*, Princeton, 1964.
J. Krishnamurti, *Commentaries on Living*, 2 vols, 1956-8.
L. L. Rai, *A History of the Arya Samaj*, New Delhi, 1967.
R. Romain, *The Life of Ramakrishna*, 1954.
S. Sastri, *History of the Brahmo Samaj*, 2 vols, 1911-12.
D. S. Sharma, *The Renaissance of Hinduism*, Varanasi, 1944.
Milton Singer (ed), *Traditional India: Structure and Change*, Philadelphia, 1959.

Index